Necessity, Essence, and Individuation

NECESSITY, ESSENCE, AND INDIVIDUATION

A Defense of Conventionalism

ALAN SIDELLE

Cornell University Press

ITHACA AND LONDON

First published 1989 by Cornell University Press.

International Standard Book Number 0-8014-2166-7
Library of Congress Catalog Card Number 89-7122
Printed in the United States of America
*Librarians: Library of Congress cataloging information
appears on the last page of the book.*

The paper in this book is acid-free and meets the guidelines for permanence and durability of the Committee on Production Guidelines for Book Longevity of the Council on Library Resources.

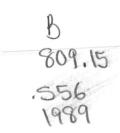

To my uncle Marty, the family philosopher,
and to Ted, fellow neo-empiricist

Essence is expressed by grammar.

—Ludwig Wittgenstein, *Philosophical Investigations* #371

Convention is the mother of necessity.

—David O. Brink*

---

*Though responsible for this quote (for my benefit), DOB should not be associated with this view.

Contents

Preface

THE NECESSARY *a posteriori* has captured the minds of recent philosophers, and for good reason. While there has been a long-standing interest in modal notions, which found its way into the development of modal logics in the middle-to-late first half of this century, there has also been a good deal of suspicion of modality. Perhaps the most familiar expression of this suspicion occurs in Quine's pronouncement that quantified modal logic commits us to 'Aristotelian essentialism', a 'jungle' from which there is supposed to be no rational escape. While Quine's writings on this matter gave rise to a good deal of discussion regarding what quantified modal logic does or does not commit us to, everyone seemed to accept that Aristotelian essentialism was a doctrine to be eschewed. The idea that objects really have essences, and this independently of any facts about how intelligent beings carve up or think about the world, was not a notion that found many defenders.

With the finding, or purported finding, however, of necessary truths that are not knowable *a priori*, matters have taken a new twist. For surely, if there are such truths, necessity and essences cannot find their homes in our conceptual schemes—if they did, all these truths, it would seem, should be analytic and *a priori*. The debates concerning modality,

then, have shifted away from questions about the commitments of modal logic and toward the question whether there
are indeed necessary *a posteriori* truths and, if so, which truths
are of this sort. And with this, essentialism, and the broader
understanding of necessity as a real-world quantity that needs
to be discovered, have become not merely reputable doc-
trines but indeed plausible ones.

Thus, even outside of discussions about necessity, we now
find philosophers making apparently unabashed use of such
notions as 'metaphysical necessity', 'essence', and 'nature', all
of which seem directed to pick out real—and indeed quite
deep—features of mind-independent reality. And insofar as it
is the task of philosophers to determine natures, or essences,
philosophy itself has come to appear, as Quine proclaimed it
to be, continuous with empirical science, and certainly not a
matter of conceptual analysis.

The necessary *a posteriori*, then, appears to provide us with
a new understanding of necessity, essences, and the nature of
metaphysics—and perhaps of philosophy as a whole. Further, it suggests a striking new picture of our relation to the
world, for we can have empirical knowledge of necessity and
essences. To borrow an overused phrase, the discovery of the
necessary *a posteriori* has 'changed the way philosophy is
done' and the way that it is viewed. Whether this revolutionary change of perspective is the right one to adopt seems
wholly a matter of whether or not there are indeed such
empirical necessary truths; current philosophical opinion
seems to favor the side of the affirmative.

This book is written in an attempt to stem the tide—but
not by arguing against the existence of the necessary *a posteriori*. What I shall be arguing is that even if we grant—as it is
coming to appear we should—that there are such truths,
none of the apparently revolutionary consequences either follows or ought to be accepted. In particular, I will argue that
there is a conventionalist account of the necessary *a posteriori*
which is both available and superior to the realist account of

such truths.[1] The conventionalist—or better, the empiricist—has traditionally maintained that all necessary truths are analytic and *a priori*. This is what makes it appear that empiricism is refuted by the finding of empirical yet necessary truths. The central tenet of the position, however, is that all necessity is *grounded* in our conventions, that there is no necessity 'out there'. The traditional version of this view is certainly the most straightforward one, but it is not the only one. Whether a conventionalist should think that all our knowledge of necessity is *a priori* depends on what sorts of conventions he thinks we have, and, as I will argue, whatever reason there is to think that there are necessary *a posteriori* truths is reason to think that (some of) our conventions are of a more complex sort, a sort that provides for the possibility of the empirical discovery of necessary truths. The necessity, however, remains firmly rooted in our conventions and re-

---

[1]As I neared the completion of the first draft of this book, I discovered to my pleasure and chagrin Paul Coppock's fine review of Nathan Salmon's *Reference and Essence* (*Journal of Philosophy* 81:261–70). In this review, Coppock presents the basic positive proposal I shall be making for the deflationary understanding of the necessary *a posteriori*, that of seeing such truths as arising from two components, one of which is necessary but analytic, and the other, empirical but contingent. Such an account, he notes, deprives the necessary *a posteriori* results of their apparent metaphysical bite (p. 268). Coppock also argues for a claim that comprises part of my argument in chapter 6, that the causal, or direct, theory of reference presupposes essentialism (though not any essentialist truths in particular: for instance, that water is essentially H_2O). Thus, the originality of my central thesis is not the principal merit I claim for this book, although, as I say, I came by it independently. Rather, the virtues I hope for it are the extended elaboration and defense of this proposal, and an exploration of the philosophical space in which the phenomenon of the necessary *a posteriori* is located. I note too that the suggestion that the general principles needed to produce necessary *a posteriori* truths might be analytic can be found in Salmon's book as well, in his Appendix II, although the idea that this could give us a successful conventionalist account does not seem to be one to which he is especially sympathetic (here I draw upon personal correspondence).

flects nothing of a mind-independent modal structure. Consequently, necessary *a posteriori* or no, we are not entitled to free talk of essences or 'natures' as if they were wholly mind-independent, real-world quantities awaiting our discovery, or of 'metaphysical' necessity, where 'metaphysical' is supposed to carry any of the weight it seems to. Nor ought we to think that, in our metaphysical inquiries, we are doing something other than conceptual analysis.

In sum, I shall be presenting and defending a conventionalist account of the necessary *a posteriori* against the apparent realist challenge it poses, arguing, thus, against real necessity and real essences. The necessary *a posteriori* neither commits us to, nor does it support, realism about necessity or essences. This is my negative claim. I also intend, however, to be presenting a positive picture. If the conventionalism I am defending is correct, it has, I hope to show, significant consequences for a number of issues of contemporary interest, including how we should understand reference, individuation, and the metaphysical status of ordinary objects and kinds. Analyticity, for instance, the whipping boy of almost four decades, should no longer have to be appealed to with fear in one's heart. Indeed, I will argue that the causal theory of reference, the heir apparent to analyticity-based semantics, actually requires significant analyticity if it is to get off the ground. Thus, the realist tandem of the necessary *a posteriori* and the causal theory of reference, far from spelling doom for empiricism, each finds itself best accounted for within an empiricist framework, somewhat ironically helping to display the strength of the resources to which the empiricist has access. By properly appreciating the dependence of necessity on analyticity, we arrive, I believe, at a significant neo-empiricist metaphysical picture that is not to be taken lightly. So much for promises.

The present book appears largely thanks to my friend and former teacher Hilary Kornblith, who, having seen some of my ideas, introduced me to John Ackerman, editor at Cornell University Press. Hilary's encouragement was especially flattering to me, as I believe he disagrees with every substantive claim I put forward herein. First thanks, then, to Hilary and John, for making this possible, and for their support.

I have been most fortunate to have received a great deal of philosophical and personal help from the following people— I hope their mention here doesn't get them into trouble:

David O. Brink, the infamous moral realist, has been by my side from start to finish. As a neighbor and friend, he is a part of my everyday life, which I can scarcely imagine without him. As a colleague, he is a continual source of philosophical discussion and of helpful and challenging comments. His encouragement has played a major role in my being able to finish this project at all.

Ted Everett first got me to acknowledge my empiricistic inclinations—to whatever extent the views expressed here are empiricist. I have learned more about philosophy through our hundreds of hours of conversation than from anyone else, and the development and articulation of my own views are immeasurably indebted to him, as is my continued interest in these issues. It is in recognition of Ted's friendship, camaraderie, and present substantive input that I dedicate this book, in part, to him.

Teresa E. Lowe and Brian Penrose played a great role in keeping my life happy and livable throughout my time at Cornell University. Their wisdom and knowledge of all aspects of popular culture provided me with endless entertainment and personal enrichment—and they made philosophical contributions too. They both live in San Francisco now, and I miss them greatly.

It is my pleasure and privilege to have worked with three outstanding philosophers: Sydney Shoemaker, Norman Kretzmann, and Robert Stalnaker. Sydney has always been extremely generous with his time, always willing to look over a piece of work or just shoot the philosophical breeze.

He read a draft of this book patiently and provided many, many valuable comments. Those familiar with Sydney's work may well detect some Shoemakerian strands of argument in this book, especially in chapter 4, the heart of the book. Though I didn't really notice this as I wrote it, it is right there, and I'm sure it is not an accident. Sydney surely deserves much credit for what is of value in this book, and I am honored to have his friendship. Bob Stalnaker is responsible for bringing to my attention the problems for my view which I attempt to address in chapter 3. The book could hardly stand without a confrontation with these difficulties, and I am grateful to Bob both for his suggestions and for the friendly manner in which he presented them. Also, insofar as this book attempts to focus attention on the larger issues within which my more particular concerns are located, I am indebted to him for displaying, by his example, how beautifully this can be done, and with what important philosophical benefits. Norman Kretzmann was ever enthusiastic and supportive, and I truly doubt that this book could have been written had it not been for his confidence in me and the perspective he brought me. To Sydney, Bob, and Norman I offer my deepest gratitude for their philosophical expertise and their kindness.

Others have made personal and philosophical contributions that have improved the quality of either this book or my life while I was writing it. I thank David M. Bernstein, William R. Carter, Richard Farr, Philip Gasper, T. H. Irwin, Scott MacDonald, Alison McIntyre, Dick Moran, Allen Rosen, Christopher Shields, Kathy Sullivan, Stephen Sullivan, Bonny Sweeney, J. D. Trout, Michael Tye, and Jennifer Whiting.

I am also indebted to Nathan Salmon and an anonymous reviewer for Cornell University Press. Their comments, criticisms, and suggestions were always fair and proved eminently helpful. I thank Deborah Hause, also at Cornell

University Press, for her patience, friendliness, and behind-the-scenes resourcefulness throughout this project.

Last, but certainly not least, I must somehow express my inexpressible indebtedness to Dana Hays. She has ever more faith in me than I have in myself, which is a constant source of motivation. Her company has kept me sane and very happy, and her intelligence, wit, encouragement, and love have all had large impact on this book. They've certainly had a great impact on me.

ALAN SIDELLE

Cambridge, Massachusetts

Necessity, Essence, and Individuation

I   *Realism and Conventionalism*

EMPIRICISTS HAVE long held that all necessary truths are both analytic and knowable *a priori*. Reasons for this view have been both epistemological and metaphysical. Our knowledge of what is necessary outstrips our knowledge of the actual, and certainly sense experience, so it is difficult to see how this knowledge could be empirical. More particularly, judgments of necessity seem always to be based on thought experiments and appeals to what we can imagine. Insofar as these methods are knowledge-producing, it would seem that they tell us, in the first instance, something about ourselves. *A priori* methods yield *a priori* knowledge, and the objects of this knowledge are not facts about the world, but analytic truths. Metaphysically, the motivation is largely puzzlement. What, in what is merely *actual*, could make it the case that some things are necessary, while others are merely contingent? What could it *be* for some state of affairs to be necessary, or for some property to be essential? What is there in these cases which makes them different from the contingent and accidental? Or, approached somewhat differently, what could an omnipotent being do to bring it about that some state of affairs was necessary, or some property essential? Insofar as these questions seem unanswerable, or deeply puzzling, we have some reason to think that modality does not find its home in the mind-independent world, but rather in us, in our ways of speaking and thinking, and thus that necessity is nothing beyond analyticity. Some further support for this position could be found from consideration of cases, the familiar examples of necessary truths being thought analytic and *a priori*, like 'Bachelors are unmarried' and 'Two plus two equals four'. This line of thought issues in what might be called 'conventionalism' about necessity, 'convention' being a catchall for mind-based contribution, and just to set this position off from what might be called 'realism', which would maintain that modality is a real, mind-independent feature of the world. Until Saul Kripke entered the picture, it would be fair to say that conventionalism was the dominant understanding of modality.

Enter Kripke and his *Naming and Necessity*.[1] Kripke has made it very plausible that there are necessary truths that are synthetic and knowable only *a posteriori*. Some of the more familiar examples are 'Hesperus is Phosporus'; 'Water is H_2O'; and 'Margaret Truman is a biological daughter of Harry and Bess Truman'. This, if correct,[2] puts the lie to the view that all necessary truths are *a priori* and analytic. But does it put the lie to conventionalism? That is, does it establish that modality is a real, mind-independent feature of the world, like wetness and dogs, perhaps a possible province for an empirical modal science?[3] This is the question from which

[1]Saul Kripke, *Naming and Necessity* (Cambridge: Harvard University Press, 1980).

[2]Whether or not Kripke and other advocates of the necessary *a posteriori* are correct is something about which I shall have very little to say, my primary focus being what we are to make of it if they *are* correct. However, the project would be odd if I did not think that a very good case had been made for the necessary *a posteriori*, and that a great many philosophers had been convinced; both of these conditions are no doubt satisfied.

[3]In posing the question this way, I hope it is clear that I am not identifying empiricism (conventionalism) with the doctrine that all necessary truths are analytic and *a priori*, but rather with the view that the source of modality is 'in us' rather than the world; it will be noted that the motiva-

this book takes off. I am not merely concerned with the question of consistency, whether or not it is possible both for conventionalism to be true and for there to be necessary *a posteriori* truths; that much I hope to establish quite quickly. What I hope to show, rather, is that even if we accept the necessary *a posteriori*, we should be conventionalists. Nothing in the acceptance of these truths, or in the arguments for them, gives us reason to be realists about modality. Indeed, I will argue, the conventionalist can give a more satisfactory account of the phenomenon of the necessary *a posteriori* than can the realist.

More generally, while the general approach of the book will take the form of arguments for conventionalism and against realism on this matter, an overarching aim is to open up discussion on how the necessary *a posteriori* ought to be understood. Although it is quite a celebrated phenomenon, there has not been much discussion of its interpretation. Its impact on the philosophical community suggests that most of us think that more is at stake here than the mere coextensionality of the necessary, the analytic, and the *a priori*; however, no one, to my knowledge, has come out and argued for a realist interpretation.[4] Thus, in arguing against realism, I

---

tions cited above work just as well for the position so specified. This is important to keep in mind for the remainder of the present chapter. In chapter 2, I will present a version of empiricism which allows for synthetic and *a posteriori* necessary truths.

[4]My guess (not that this matters much) is that such arguments are not to be found because most philosophers take for granted that the necessary *a posteriori* establishes realism. They may do so because they mistakenly identify conventionalism with its most common form, namely, the view that all necessary truths are analytic and *a priori* (in which case conventionalism would be trivially refuted), or (perhaps on the basis of this identification) because they underestimate the resources of the conventionalist position. Another possibility—perhaps the same as the last—is simply that, given the empirical nature of the necessary *a posteriori*, it may seem plain that these truths must be so simply by corresponding to facts in the world. Nothing of importance, however, hinges on this speculation

might be thought to be going out on a limb. To this I have two replies. First, as I try to suggest in the section after next, even in the absence of explicit discussions of the matter, there is a way of approaching and talking about modal issues that is now both common and hard to make sense of if we do not suppose something like realism to be implicit. No one with whom I have discussed these issues finds realism about modality alien, or believes it to be uncommon; indeed, most suppose that it is the straightforward understanding of the necessary *a posteriori*. After all, if these truths cannot be known through reflection, but need to be discovered by empirical investigation, doesn't it seem plain, at least on the face of it, that they concern mind-independent features of reality? Again, it is difficult to understand the stir caused by Kripke's findings if it is not because they seem to support real essentialism and a metaphysical picture of modality. It is no doubt interesting that not all necessary truths are analytic and *a priori*, but if there is metaphysical punch here, it has got to be in the *why*. Second, as I suggested above, while I am arguing against realism, this can be seen as a straightforward way of starting a discussion about what to make of the necessary *a posteriori*. Even if no one had any firm opinions on the matter, as I said, it is a matter that certainly merits discussion, and about which there seem to be two obvious positions. Since I believe one of them and not the other, this is how I shall argue, and no one in particular need be thought of as my opponent.[5] Of course, if conventionalism were obvious, and

---

(though, I may add, it is not part of my speculation that any of this is typically articulate).

[5]While I am not familiar with any literature that argues for realism on the basis of the necessary *a posteriori*, there are, to be sure, independent proponents. Frege and the early Russell may be of this stripe (although their concerns are with the nature of logic as such, and not directly with necessity). More vehemently so, perhaps, was Arthur Pap; see his *Semantics and Necessary Truth* (New Haven: Yale University Press, 1958). A more recent presentation can be found in Robert Adams, "Has It Been Proved That All

everyone believed it—even in the face of the new findings—
it might be superfluous to write a book defending it (although even articulation of widely held positions has its
place). But if experience is any indication, not everyone is a
conventionalist, and certainly not in the face of the necessary
a posteriori.

Articulating the Dispute: Some First Shots

I have briefly indicated that the position I call 'realism
about necessity' maintains that modality is a real, mind-
independent feature of reality, that (at least some of)[6] the
truths that are necessary are so because the states of affairs
they depict are, as a matter of the way the world is, quite
independently of the ways we talk and think about them,
necessary. Just as we think that we have nothing to do with
the fact that Kareem Abdul-Jabbar is taller than Willie Shoemaker,[7] so we have nothing to do with the fact that water is

---

Existence Is Contingent?" *American Philosophical Quarterly* 8 (1971): 284–
91, and "Divine Necessity," *Journal of Philosophy* 80 (1983): 741–51. I shall
not be discussing these works directly, not because they do not merit
attention, but because my primary focus is on what to make of the necessary *a posteriori*. Even if a complete and satisfactory conventionalism could
not be worked out, I would still wish to argue (1) that no new worries are
raised by the necessary *a posteriori* and (2) that this phenomenon in particular ought to receive a conventionalistic treatment.

[6]I enter this qualification because even a realist might accept that *some*
necessary truths get their modal force through our conventions. Realists
like Pap and Adams would presumably not be of this sort, but someone
who thought that we had to realistically understand the necessary *a posteriori* might think that, for more familiar analytic necessary truths, conventionalism provided a satisfactory account. The situation might be com-
pared to the related controversy in the theory of reference; advocates of
causal or direct theories of reference need not maintain that there are (or
could be) no terms that gain their reference through analytically given
meanings, but only that many—presumably, an interesting many—do
not.

[7]Those of us who are not idealists, at any rate.

necessarily H_2O or that Margaret Truman is essentially a biological daughter of Harry and Bess Truman.[8] It just so happens that water's being H_2O enjoys a modal status that the relative heights of Kareem and Willie do not. All of these are equally facts in the world, independent of our conventions or our evidence for them.

While this characterization hopefully gets across something of what is at issue between realists and conventionalists, one might wonder why we couldn't, perhaps more informatively, draw the issue another way.[9] Why not say that realists believe that there are true essential predications, or true statements beginning with 'Necessarily'? This, of course, draws a different line, between what we might call 'necessitarians' and 'anti-necessitarians'. Conventionalists, of course, are free to believe that there are true statements of the sort described. Where they differ from realists is over the grounds of this necessity, or, to borrow Armstrong's phrase, over the 'truth-makers' for modal statements.[10] Keeping this in mind, though, may help to make the issue clearer.

This suggests another reformulation. Perhaps realists and conventionalists disagree over the truth of certain counterfactuals. After all, if the conventionalist claims that *we* are somehow responsible for necessity and essence, isn't he claiming that if we had different conventions, what is necessary would be different? To put things more particularly, couldn't we say that the conventionalist affirms, while the realist denies, that if we had decided to talk or think differently, then water might have only contingently been H_2O?

---

[8]Again, I do not mean to presuppose that these things *are* necessary or essential; for simplicity and familiarity, however, I shall continue to draw my examples from the cases presented in the literature.

[9]While I will not find any of the following attempts wholly satisfactory, discussing them may at least help to dispel certain misconceptions about what conventionalists must be committed to.

[10]Or, alternatively, over the 'necessity-makers' for statements that do not themselves make modal claims.

I do not think that this will do. While the conventional-ist—as well as the realist—will agree that with different conventions, the statement 'Necessarily, water is H_2O' could be false, the conventionalist is no more obliged than the realist to affirm the mere 'contingent' necessity of water's being H_2O. For when we discuss counterfactuals, we are speaking our actual language, guided by our actual conventions. If it is a convention of ours that nothing in any possible situation counts as water if it is not composed of H_2O,[11] then this very convention tells us that in the subclass of possible situations in which we have different conventions, still, nothing counts as water that is not H_2O: that is, that it is necessary that water is H_2O. The situation is no different here than for analytically necessary truths; hypothesizing different conventions does not make the conventionalist deny the necessity of what he claims our conventions make necessary.

It seems, then, that there will be no simple way of characterizing the issue in terms of disagreements about what is, or might be, necessary. A better attempt might be the way realist/anti-realist disputes are sometimes drawn in other contexts, in terms of evidence.[12] The realist, then, may claim that the truth of issues about what is necessary, or essential, might, in principle, outstrip all the possible evidence we could have on the matter. The conventionalist—or 'anti-realist', here—would deny that, claiming that when all the evidence was in, there are no outstanding facts about which we can be wrong. Thus, in the 'evidentiary' limit, any remaining disputes must be purely verbal, with each side mak-

---

[11]I do not mean to suggest that the conventionalist should maintain that it is analytic that water is H_2O; as will become clear presently, there are more complex ways in which what is described here could be a matter of convention.

[12]For an example of this way of drawing the issue in ethics, see David O. Brink, "Moral Realism and the Skeptical Arguments from Disagreement and Queerness," *Australasian Journal of Philosophy*, 62 (June 1984): 111–25. The general strategy may be properly attributed to Charles Pierce.

ing true claims, but with different content.[13] While there is some merit in this position, it is not completely clear that either side needs to accept these claims. Realists might think that as things turn out, we cannot be wrong in the limit (this may depend on how the limit is specified),[14] and the conventionalist may think that there is room for possible error, even in the limit (see note 13). This will especially be the case if the conventionalist thinks that empirical matters can enter into the determination of what is necessary (as I will suggest he should in the case of the necessary *a posteriori*), or if he thinks that even in the limit, there can be disputes about what our conventions are. Thus, while this 'outstripping' test is a useful guideline, it should not be thought of as definitive.[15]

[13]Things may get a bit complicated here. If we think that, even in fairly extreme cases, people are not in charge of their own ideolects, then we may not be able to characterize these disputes as merely verbal—they may concern disagreements, say, about the intentions of the majority of speakers, or 'experts' of one's language, or even, indeed, about whether speakers are answerable to the whole community. These issues, then, would have to be reckoned a part of the total evidence, and it is not clear that even a conventionalist about necessity must maintain that about these apparently empirical issues, we could not be wrong in the limit. The conventionalist about necessity need not be an anti-realist about everything, and insofar as empirical issues might enter into questions about what is necessary (as in, for instance, questions about what our conventions are), it is not clear that the conventionalist must maintain that we cannot be wrong, even in the limit, about questions of necessity. (It will become clear in the next chapter how, in the case of the necessary *a posteriori*, further empirical issues can become involved while not compromising the conventionalist.)

[14]For some worries about this characterization, see Michael Devitt, "Dummett's Anti-Realism," *Journal of Philosophy* 80 (1983): 73–99.

[15]At this point, it might be useful to enter what should already be clear, but might still be on some readers' minds, that what I am calling 'realism about necessity' is not to be equated with what is often called 'modal realism', a view about possible worlds usually associated with David Lewis (see, for the most recent defense, his *On the Plurality of Worlds* [Oxford and New York: Basil Blackwell, 1986]. Lewis's position—roughly, that other possible worlds are real worlds of just the same sort as ours, except that we aren't there—is neither necessary nor sufficient for realism about necessity. While the strongest conventionalist will presumably want to maintain

In the face of this lack of success, some skeptics may wonder if there is anything to dispute once parties have agreed or disagreed over questions about what is necessary.[16] I hope that there is enough intuitive content in my first characterization to make this skepticism seem unwarranted. Realists and conventionalists disagree over the grounds of necessity, over what makes the necessary necessary. Perhaps we could say that they differ over the 'metaphysical depth' of necessity. Consider: I introduce the term 'squg' as short for 'round and red'. It will then be a necessary truth that whatever is squg is red. Is this a deep metaphysical fact about squgs? The conventionalist will say that it is not, that there is nothing more to it than our adoption of a certain way of speaking, and, indeed, the realist need not object (see note 5). But now consider: Through our investigation of gold, we learn empirically that gold necessarily has atomic number 79. The realist will maintain that this is a deep fact about gold, just the sort of thing that we traditionally think of metaphysics as being about. It is what gold *is*, and it is not a matter of our having decided to use 'gold' as short for 'whatever has atomic number 79'. That this is the essence of gold is 'out there' in the world. A conventionalist, on the other hand, would need to either make out the case that, appearances notwithstanding, it is analytic that gold has atomic number 79, or that, in

---

some sort of linguistic or conceptual account of the nature of possible worlds, the issue with which I am concerned is more about what it is in virtue of which items have the modal features they do, an issue which, as I hope will become clear, has more to do with individuation than with the standing of possible worlds. The two issues are thus orthogonal, and one need not be a Lewisian realist in order to be a realist about necessity; indeed, I think that many who would disavow Lewis' position in the strongest possible terms are yet realists, in my sense.

[16]One last alternative, which I have omitted from the discussion so as not to belabor the point, would be that realists accept, while conventionalists reject, *de re* modalities. As should become clear in chapter 3, I do not see that a sophisticated conventionalist is debarred from embracing modality *de re*.

some other way, it is our conventions that give the modal force to gold's having this deep structure, so that there is no more depth to this fact about gold than there is to the necessary roundness of squgs.

Having said this much about the disagreement between realists and conventionalists about necessity, let me try to present a picture of modality and modal inquiry that may help to further clarify things, and to explain why it is that I think that, whether they know it or not, many philosophers are indeed realists, at least when it comes to the necessary *a posteriori*.

Realism about Necessity: A Picture[17]

Anyone familiar with the necessary *a posteriori* should find the following a familiar account of empirical modal inquiry. Discussions here usually occur in connection with causal theories of reference.[18] The reason is simple: If we pick out the objects of our inquiries by means of analytically associated definite descriptions, as traditional theories have it, then the modal boundaries of the objects are already set, and there is nothing further to be discovered. According to the causal theory, however, we can refer to these items (individuals and kinds being the usual examples) directly, without these analytic intermediaries, descriptions serving at most to 'fix the

---

[17]In calling this a picture, I do not mean to suggest, as is sometimes done in 'picture-talk', that what is contained here cannot be expressed by means of propositions, or that there are not propositional differences between those with the realist picture and conventionalists. It is rather that sometimes we can grasp what is at stake in some dispute by suggesting how the disputants look at things. There is no hint here that no propositional representation of such a dispute is possible.

[18]The classic texts here are Kripke, *Naming and Necessity*, and Hilary Putnam, "The Meaning of 'Meaning'," in *Mind, Language and Reality* (Cambridge: Cambridge University Press, 1975).

reference' of our terms.[19] Thus, the causal theory gives us a way to get at an object[20] while leaving it undetermined what its essence or necessary features might be.

Now, once we have got hold (so to speak) of an object in this way, we may pursue various questions about it, asking, in particular, about its essential features. Does Margaret Truman have her origin essentially? What is the essence of water? Is John essentially human? We may even ask 'What is the nature of this?' or 'of this stuff?', the demonstratives emphasizing the apparently *de re* and language(mind)-independent nature of our inquiry. Are these not squarely metaphysical matters? We cannot be asking about our concepts or linguistic associations, for there are none. 'What is essential to gold?' cannot be glossed as 'What is the definition of 'gold'?'—not, that is, unless we think the answer is 'Nothing.' By pursuing these modal inquiries in a context where analyticity is thought to be nonexistent, or, at least, not pertinent to the issue, one certainly seems to be asking about a mind-independent modal structure of reality.

If one thought that necessity was analyticity, one would find it simply idle to ask such questions where it was being supposed that meanings were not in the offing, except, perhaps, for iconoclastic purposes. And, once one supposes that necessity is not just analyticity, in these days of the necessary *a posteriori* when positive answers are being given to the above inquiries, one would expect positive-answering conventionalists to go out of their way a bit, to explain that while they are advocating non-analytic necessities, still they

[19]See Kripke, *Naming and Necessity*, pp. 55–56, for his introduction of the reference-fixing/meaning-giving distinction.
[20]Unless it is specified otherwise, I use words such as 'object', 'item', and 'thing' to cover not only individuals but any suitable subject of modal inquiry; this will simplify matters, as we do not have convenient terms to cover individuals as well as kinds.

are not being 'real essentialists',[21] and modalities still find their home in our conventions. Surely, in the face of the necessary *a posteriori*, some disclaimer would be called for, insofar as the standard understanding of conventionalism was that necessary truths were all analytic and *a priori*, and these empirical inquiries into modality at least seem to be so object-directed.

A parallel: Suppose it came to be a philosophical commonplace for people to advocate moral rules that, on their faces, prescribed actions that failed to maximize utility, even in the long run. Unless at least some of these philosophers offered explanations of how this was compatible with, or actually best accounted for by, utilitarianism, it would be reasonable to suppose that the prevailing philosophical moral opinion was deontological. In the absence of similar disclaimers or explanations in our present case, it seems reasonable to suppose that, if only implicitly, the prevailing philosophical modal opinion is realist.

The analogy may be thought a bad one, since non–utility-maximizing rules so plainly look deontological, while the sort of modal inquiry described above, even with positive results being advocated, may not seem so plainly realist. Well, it certainly isn't plainly conventionalist, and the contrasts that are drawn with more traditional pictures, the emphasis that is placed on these inquiries' not being matters of conceptual analysis, the emphasis placed on its being the *objects* we are finding out about, and, finally, the supposed importance of the results—all point to a realist understanding of the nature of the inquiry, and of the necessary *a posteriori*. A few examples may help to bring this out.

In the traditional empiricist picture, the way we go about modal inquiry is by trying to see whether we can imagine a situation in which it would be correct to assert the negation

[21]For more on real essentialism and its contrast with nominal essentialism, see pp. 18–24.

of a proposed necessary truth. This is a way in which we can find out the limits of our concepts, our rules of application. Judgments about what would be true in such imagined cases are called 'intuitions', and since our rules are the determinants of what is necessary, consulting our intuitions to find out what rules we are employing is *the* method of modal inquiry. Here, then, is a quote from Putnam:

> We can perfectly well imagine experiences that would convince us (and that would make it rational to believe that) water *isn't* H_2O. In that sense, it is conceivable that water isn't H_2O. It is conceivable, but it isn't logically possible! Conceivability is no proof of logical possibility. . . . Human intuition has no privileged access to metaphysical possibility.[22]

Anyone who accepts the necessary *a posteriori* must be at least willing to accept something like this, conventionalists included.[23] This is because intuitions tell us what is or isn't analytic, and, by hypothesis here, what is necessary will outstrip what is analytic. However, no one who thought that empiricism was basically right, or that it could be adequate to the task of explaining the necessary *a posteriori*, would go out of his way to make the point Putnam is making—at least, not unless it was just to acknowledge a bad-*looking* consequence for conventionalism, with the aim of then explaining away this unfortunate appearance. This is not Putnam's aim. He is clearly trying to contrast what he takes to be the current situation with what the more traditional view says. And in emphasizing this negative point about human intuition, he similarly emphasizes the positive role of the empirical, and presents a picture of the nature of modal space as something that is mind-independent, 'out there', awaiting our discoveries.

---

[22]Putnam, "The Meaning of 'Meaning'," p. 233.
[23]My account of just to what extent what Putnam says is true will be found in chapter 4.

If I may stay with Putnam for a moment, his famous Twin Earth discussion of water provides another example.[24] Putnam has us imagine that there is a place, Twin Earth, which is just like our Earth except that the stuff there that fills lakes, is used for washing and making lemonade, is rained, and so on, has a complicated chemical structure, abbreviated as 'XYZ', which is not H_2O. Putnam tells us that the stuff on Twin Earth is not water, and by extrapolation—thinking of Twin Earth now as the possible world relevant for trying to decide whether there can be water that is not H_2O—that water is necessarily H_2O. He is not, of course, claiming that it is analytic that water is H_2O; he is quite concerned to maintain that this is an empirical discovery (pp. 225, 232–33). Putnam here seems to be clearly maintaining that we have discovered, of water, that it is necessarily H_2O. This is a fact about water, and not at all of our making. It is a property of this liquid, which we happen to call 'water', that it stands in the *cross-world* relation of 'same liquid' to all and only wholes composed of H_2O (pp. 232–33). That is, water is *essentially* H_2O; that is its *nature* (p. 233).

Here again, as I have suggested and will explain presently, much of what is advocated here can be asserted by a conventionalist. But certainly not with this emphasis. For the conventionalist, cross-world sameness relations are not just out there, waiting to be discovered, and they are certainly not deep metaphysical features of the objects that stand in them. It may indeed need to be discovered that water is H_2O, but if water is essentially H_2O, this is going to have something to do with our intentions in using 'water'. Again, talk of 'natures' would at least be euphemistic for a conventionalist; without deflationary asides, such talk, and talk of 'what it is to *be*' something, seem clearly intended to make claims about mind-independent features of reality.

This is echoed by (or actually, is an echo of, if we are

[24]Putnam, "The Meaning of 'Meaning'," pp. 223–25, 230–33.

concerned with temporal priority here) a remark of Kripke's: "Let us suppose that scientists have investigated the nature of gold and have found that it is part of the very nature of this substance, so to speak, that it have atomic number 79."[25] While the emphasis is not quite so strong, the suggestion is still that the discovery of modality is an empirical matter, and something that does not require conceptual reflection or depend on our conventions in the least. Perhaps a clearer example can be found in Kripke's defense of the essentiality of origin, in which he asks, "How could a person originating from different parents, from a totally different sperm and egg, be *this very woman?*"[26] The emphasis, again, is on the essence as a real and deep feature of the object, not something that is to be explained by the way we talk or think. It is also noteworthy that Kripke rejects a 'nominal essence' interpretation of what he is advocating, thus making a more metaphysical, realist reading of his understanding of the matter fairly straightforward.[27]

These few examples should be enough to get across the flavor of how these matters are discussed; the emphases, contrasts, and lack of disclaimers or deflationary asides are common throughout the literature. It is acceptable to respond to imagination-based objections to one's theses by claiming that one is advocating a metaphysical necessity, and not merely something analytic, and discussions about what is essential, or what 'makes something an *F*', are almost never presented as matters the facts of which depend crucially upon our conventions. Modal inquiry is regularly taken to be about the world, and not about, or dependent on, us. Even if it is difficult to say just what realism about necessity and essence is, beyond saying that it is the view that what is necessary and what is essential are mind-independent features of the world,

[25]Kripke, *Naming and Necessity*, p. 124.
[26]Ibid., p.113 The emphasis is Kripke's.
[27]Ibid., p.115, n. 58.

I hope these paradigms at least bring out a sense of two different ways in which modal issues may be approached and understood. What is it that we are basically learning about when we progress in these issues? Our concepts, our rules for speech and thought? Or metaphysically deep facts about the objects investigated? And if I have succeeded in drawing this contrast, I hope I have also succeeded in suggesting how natural realism here is, at least in the case of the necessary *a posteriori*. This would help explain why nobody has found it necessary to argue against conventionalism on this basis, and may also suggest to some that, even if they have not explicitly thought about it, they at least incline toward a realist interpretation of the phenomenon. At the very least, I hope it is clear why I think conventionalism is a doctrine that needs to be reestablished.

One final thought on the matter of emphasis and depth. I am not suggesting that there is a mere attitudinal difference between conventionalists and realists. Rather, there is an attitudinal difference because there is a doctrinal disagreement, and it is this latter that I hoped to bring out by noting the metaphysical importance that many philosophers place on current modal inquiry. For if the realist is right, we are finding out, say, what water *is*—the deepest fact about water— and someone who thinks that Twin Earth XYZ is water (supposing he knows our water to be H_2O) is just wrong. He is making a factual error, and the sort of error upon which many important philosophical mistakes can be based.[28] If, on the other hand, the conventionalist is right, facts about essence and necessity have no more metaphysical depth than facts about what our conventions are (although, according to the conventionalist, this turns out to be the extent of the depth of metaphysics). Nobody finds it very deep that it is necessary that bachelors are unmarried, and if one is not a

---

[28]Real essences can be something of a philosophical weapon: 'You misunderstand the very *nature* of the thing!'

realist about, or because of, the necessary *a posteriori*, one should think that those necessities are of just the same sort. The above person who thinks that XYZ is water is not just wrong; he is either using 'water' differently than (most of?) the rest of us, or has mistaken beliefs about the rules we in his community have for using the term 'water'. Metaphysical debate, then, for the conventionalist, is not a matter of trying to see deeply into the structure of mind-independent reality, but is rather a matter of trying to clarify the way we actually speak and think, and perhaps of negotiating which ways of doing this would be to our best advantage. This is not to say that for the conventionalist metaphysics (or, if one insists, 'metaphysics') is not a deep and difficult enterprise, but the depth is of a dramatically different sort than the realist has in mind. These differences in emphasis, then, seem to be good indications of the modal positions a philosopher holds; and it should also be clear why I think the differences between realists and conventionalists about necessity and essence have such bearing on what philosophy is about and how it should be done.[29] In the next two chapters, I will show how there could be conventions that would generate necessary *a posteriori* truths, including those which have been regarded as the best candidates for such truths. This being so, the fact of there being necessary *a posteriori* truths is not incompatible with conventionalism; if these truths are to establish his position, the realist must argue that his account of them is better than that of the conventionalists. And in chapter 4, I will argue that no such argument is forthcoming.

An Historical Postscript

I conclude these preliminary remarks with a quick glance at some of Locke's remarks on these matters, in part to show

---

[29]It is no accident if these remarks mirror some of the thoughts Carnap

that Locke's central commitment was indeed to conventionalism as I have described it, rather than to the narrower doctrine that all necessary truths are analytic (thus strengthening the claim that this is indeed what is fundamental to the empiricist's position), but also because I think Locke is important for seeing the systematic significance of modal matters. I use him, then, to draw a few connections that we will want to draw upon later, as well as to indicate some of the importance of our present inquiry.

Locke is well known to us in this connection for his distinction between real and nominal essences:

> The measure and boundary of each Sort or Species, whereby it is constituted that particular sort, and distinguished from others, is that we call its Essence. . . .[T]he nominal Essence of Gold, is that complex Idea the word Gold stands for, let it be, for instance, a Body yellow, of a certain weight, malleable, fusible, and fixed. But the real Essence is the constitution of the insensible part of that Body, on which those Qualities, and all the other Properties of Gold depend.[30]

Although there is no incompatibility in this passage between a species' having a nominal and a real essence, there is a question of priority, of which 'essence' it is that truly provides the boundary of a species, and it is this question to which this chapter of the *Essay* is directed. And Locke, of course, takes it to be the nominal essence—"our ranking and distinguishing natural Substances into Species consists in the Nominal Essences the mind makes" (11). For this reason, we may call Locke a 'nominal essentialist', and those who think the boundaries are provided in nature itself 'real essentialists'.

---

presents in his "Empiricism, Semantics and Ontology," in *Meaning and Necessity* (Chicago: University of Chicago Press, 1947).

[30]John Locke, *Essay Concerning Human Understanding*, ed. P.H. Nidditch (New York: Oxford, 1975), bk. 3, chap. 6; see especially sec. 2. All references to follow will be from book 3, chapter 6; I will indicate the section in parentheses in the text.

Locke also here makes the key link between essences and boundaries. If essences determine these boundaries, then the ontological status of the sorts depends on that of the essences. If essences are the products of convention and mentality, so then are the species they delimit: "It being different Essences alone, that make different Species, 'tis plain, that they who make those abstract Ideas, which are the nominal Essences, do thereby make the Species or Sorts. . . . All which determination of the Species, 'tis plain, depends on the Understanding of Man, making this or that complex Idea" (35). For convenience, we may call this view 'nominalism about kinds' or say that Locke believes only in nominal, as opposed to real, kinds. And if we believe that individuals have essences that determine their boundaries—and so them *themselves*—then, if we believe these individual essences also to be but nominal, we will believe that (these) individuals are nominal existents, or in Locke's words, "the Workmanship of the Understanding" (12). Of course, the nominalist as opposed to the realist is not claiming here that somehow we produce species (or individuals) out of thin air—the nominalist is not an idealist. Rather, he is claiming that while there are real features of the world out there, none of them are, considering the contribution of the world itself, essential to anything: we get essences, as such, only from our methods of carving up the world. But if species (individuals) are what they are in virtue of their essences, and their essences, as such, are not 'out there', then Locke is pointing out that we must say that to that extent, the species (individuals) *themselves* are not, as such, 'out there'. If Locke is right in drawing these connections, then our general inquiry into necessity is of more interest than may at first be supposed, insofar as essences are the boundaries of species (individuals). Upon the real or conventional nature of essences—necessary properties—rests the real or conventional nature of species (individuals). One's views about necessity may have far-reaching metaphysical consequences.

We have, then, Locke's distinction between real and nominal essences, his advocacy of nominal essentialism, and his concomitant view that the sorts and species of things are "the Workmanship of the Understanding." We may now ask: Why was Locke a nominal essentialist?

On one currently popular interpretation, Locke's position was not fundamentally metaphysical at all, but rather resulted from his epistemological and semantic views. Locke thought that words gain meaning and reference by being associated with our ideas. But we have no ideas—no knowledge—of the deep hidden structures of things which are their real essences. Consequently, our species terms cannot pick out things according to these "inward contrivances," but must rather be associated with ideas of their more manifest features. On this view, metaphysically speaking, Locke is actually a real essentialist: it is just that our words cannot divide the world according to the boundaries set by the real essences. There are indeed real species, but the species of which we can speak, bounded as they are merely by the more sensible properties of things, are but nominal.[31]

Though I have not the time to argue it fully here (along with the fact that it has been done better than I could elsewhere),[32] I do not think this can be the correct explanation of Locke's view. I will settle for a lengthy quote in which Locke quite explicitly states that even if we were epistemically better off, species would still be creatures of the mind:

> A silent and striking Watch, are but one Species, to those who have but one name for them: but he that has the name Watch for one, and Clock for the other, and distinct complex Ideas,

[31]This account is more popular in informal discussion and classroom presentations than it is in print. It can be found, though, in J. L. Mackie, "Locke's Anticipation of Kripke," *Analysis* 34 (1974): 177–80, and Richard Boyd, "Scientific Realism and Naturalistic Epistemology," *Proceedings of the Philosophy of Science Association*, vol. 2 (1980): 640–45.

[32]See Michael Ayers's lovely article "Locke versus Aristotle on Natural Kinds," *Journal of Philosophy* 78 (1981): 247–72.

to which these names belong, to him they are different Species. It will be said, perhaps, that the inward contrivance and constitution is different between these two, which the Watchmaker has a clear Idea of. And yet, 'tis plain, they are but one Species to him, when he has but one name for them. *For what is sufficient in the inward contrivance to make a new Species?* There are some Watches, that are made with four wheels, others with five: Is this a specifik difference to the Workman? . . . Are any, or all of these enough to make a specifik difference to the Workman, that knows each of these, and several other different contrivances, in the internal Constitutions of Watches? 'Tis certain, each of these hath a real difference from the rest: But whether it be an essential, a specifik difference or no, relates only to the complex Idea, to which the name Watch is given. . . . Just thus, I think, it is in natural things. (39, emphasis mine)

It seems clear from this passage that Locke's nominal essentialism does not arise from an epistemological skepticism concerning our abilities to know of "the inward contrivance of things."[33] Watch-makers do know of such contrivances, but watch-species are still creatures of the mind, and the final line of the passage embodies Locke's view that even if we could know the inner contrivances of natural objects and defined our terms accordingly, we would still fail to be dividing things into real species. The problem is not epistemological, and Locke is not a closet real essentialist.[34]

The passage also suggests more positively why Locke *is* a nominal essentialist. "For what is sufficient in the inward Contrivance to make a new Species?" Locke is not denying that there may be real, deep, and explanatory similarities among watches, or natural things, but he is puzzled as to

---

[33]This is not, of course, to say that Locke was not a skeptic here, but only that it cannot explain his being a nominal essentialist.

[34]Locke, of course, does talk about real essences, but he makes it clear that such talk only makes sense after the nominal essences are in place. See bk. 3, chap. 6, sec. 4. See also Ayers, "Locke versus Aristotle," p. 260.

how this fact could make the properties in question, or any-thing else, essential, how it could provide the sort of meta-physical boundary that an essence is supposed to be. And this puzzlement, in turn, I believe, is motivated by a suspicion of real necessity. Boundaries are essences, essences are necessary properties, but there is no real necessity, so no real essences, and so no real boundaries. Locke's perplexity over bound-aries and essences, and his positive view that we must pro-vide them, I propose, is informed by his belief that our ideas, or conventions (intentions), are the only source for the modal force that they carry.

> 'Tis necessary for me to be as I am . . . but there is nothing I have, is essential to me. . . . Color or shape. . . Reason or Memory . . . no nor life . . . [n]one of these are essential . . . to any individual whatsoever, till the Mind refers it to some Sort or Species of things, and then presently, accord-ing to the abstract Idea of that Sort, something is found essen-tial. (4)

> It would be absurd to ask, Whether a thing really existing, wanted anything essential to it. Or could it be demanded, Whether this made an essential or specifik difference or no; since we have no measure of essential or specifik, but our abstract Ideas? (5)

Locke seems to just not know what someone could mean if he said something was essential, but that this was not so simply as a matter of the rules of speech (abstract Ideas). I don't know if this constitutes a good argument (see chap. 4, pp. 114–20), but I think it expresses a deep puzzlement that forms the basis of the conventionalist's position. If I am right about this, Locke's nominal essentialism is not driven by his epistemological and semantic views, but by a grave meta-physical doubt, supplemented perhaps by success in seeing how one *is* able to understand talk of essences if one focuses instead on the complex ideas that govern our speech.

At this point we may also note that while Locke does think that our species terms are annexed to complex ideas that constitute their definitions, and so probably thought that all necessary truths were analytic, this is not at all essential to his thinking that essences must be explained conventionally. No doubt, this is the simplest, most straightforward way for necessity to be explained in terms of our speech (ideas), but if it is not the only way—and it is the burden of the next two chapters to show that it is not—this should be perfectly acceptable to Locke *qua* nominal essentialist. What is important is not that all necessary (essence-stating) truths be analytic, but that their modal force be explained in terms of *us*, in terms of our carving up of the world, and not in terms of an independently existing modal structure of reality.

My aims in this section, it should be apparent, have not been especially historical. Largely, Locke's distinction between real and nominal essences provides a useful framework within which to cast the dispute between realists and conventionalists about necessity. By looking at this interpretation of Locke, perhaps we can better see that the dispute is not over whether all necessary truths are analytic or not, but over the nature of necessity and the grounds of essences. The conventionalist claims that these grounds are to be found in our conventions, and while it may be most obvious to think of this as equating necessity with analyticity, if there is indeed a way for there to be conventions which would give rise to synthetic, *a posteriori* necessary truths, this is well within the conventionalist's position. The necessary *a posteriori*, of itself, is nothing to which a conventionalist must in principle object. And insofar as Locke is the granddaddy of empiricism, it ought to be acceptable to say that the basic empiricist position on necessity is that it is not a creature of the world, but is rather a creature of the understanding. If this is compatible with necessity *a posteriori*, then empiricism is. Finally, Locke is important to us for the connections he draws between essences, boundaries, and the ontological status of the items that have these essences. This sheds some light on the significance of investigating necessity, and will be important later on as we try to explore and make use of the further metaphysical reaches of the conventionalist, or empiricist, position.

Now that we have a better idea of what is at stake, and what the disputants claim, it is time to see how the conventionalist can accept the claim that there are necessary *a posteriori* truths without abandoning his claim that all necessity is grounded in our conventions. How can the conventionalist explain the necessary *a posteriori*?

2 How to Be a Modern-Day Conventionalist

BEFORE I BEGIN to respond to the realist challenge posed by the necessary *a posteriori*, it may be useful to briefly review the phenomenon itself. The familiar examples one finds include 'Hesperus is (the same planet as) Phosphorus', 'Cicero is Tully', 'Margaret Truman is a biological daughter of Bess Truman', 'Water is H_2O' and 'Gold is the element with atomic number 79'. These may be crudely divided into two groups—(synthetic) *identity* statements (between rigid designators), and statements of *essential* properties. The first two examples belong to the former group, the third to the latter, and the last two are presented sometimes as property-identity statements and sometimes as statements of the essence of a natural kind.[1]

In the case of identity statements, Kripke has revived an argument of Ruth Barcan Marcus's to the effect that if an identity holds, it holds necessarily.[2] Kripke puts the point intuitively: "What pairs (x,y) could be counterexamples [to

---

[1] In the case of properties (at least), it is not clear that there is any difference here, so long as we are considering the whole essence, i.e., everything that is essential.

[2] Ruth Barcan Marcus, "The Identity of Individuals in a Strict Functional Calculus of Second Order," *Journal of Symbolic Logic* 12 (1947): 12–15.

the necessity of identity, that is, $(x)(y)(x = y) \supset \Box \, (x = y)]$?
Not pairs of distinct objects, for then the antecedent is false;
nor any pair of an object and itself, for then the consequent is
true."[3] An object and itself are necessarily identical, while
any two distinct objects are not identical to begin with.[4] To
this, Kripke adds the familiar point that there are true empirical identity statements, and thus, with a caveat about rigid
designation, that these will be necessary *a posteriori* truths,
Hesperus and Cicero again being the familiar subjects.

For essential predications, the arguments are a bit more
complex. It is clear, of course, that if there are true essential
predications, then they express necessary properties; what is
at issue is whether there *are* such true predications. Strong
cases have been made, however, in at least two general
categories—predications of origin and of deep microstructure.[5]

Kripke gives "something like a proof" of the essentiality of
origin (p. 114, n. 56), arguing, roughly, that any alternative
origin for an object could have been the origin of a distinct
object, and thus that if we suppose our original object could
have had a different origin, we would need to identify it, in
that world, with this other object, violating the necessity of
identity (or more properly, of distinctness).[6] More infor-
mally, Kripke argues: "How could a person originating from

[3]Kripke, *Naming and Necessity*, p. 3. Brackets are mine.
[4]This argument is not wholly uncontroversial. For an interesting interpretation of identity statements, and an argument against the necessity of
identity, see Panayot Butchvarov, *Being Qua Being* (Bloomington: Indiana
University Press, 1979), chapter 2, especially pp. 72–75. See also Allan
Gibbard, "Contingent Identity," *Journal of Philosophical Logic* 4 (1975):
187–222.
[5]I by no means wish to suggest that these are the only categories in
which cases can be made—only that they are the most familiar.
[6]For further discussion of this argument, see Nathan Salmon, "How *Not*
to Derive Essentialism from the Theory of Reference," *Journal of Philosophy* 76 (1979): 703–25, and Graham Forbes, "Origin and Identity," *Philosophical Studies* 37 (1980): 353–62.

a totally different sperm and egg, be *this very woman?* One can imagine, *given* the woman, that various things in her life could have changed. . . . But it is harder to imagine her born of different parents. It seems to me that anything coming from a different origin would not be this object."[7] Along these lines is the thought that in order to get something's possibilities, you must first have the thing itself. There is a strong intuitive pull to the idea that one can go back only as far as the origin of a thing and that the origin itself could not have been different—it is the starting point after which alternative possibilities may begin. So these considerations support the essentiality of origin. However, it is clearly an *a posteriori* matter who one's parents were. It is no part of the concept of Margaret Truman, if such a concept there be, that her mother was Bess Truman. Failure to know who her mother was is no linguistic failure. Thus, (true) statements of the origins of material objects have a strong claim to being necessary *a posteriori.* Similarly, Kripke and Putnam have argued that statements expressing the deep microstructural features of substances are necessary *a posteriori.* Such statements certainly seem empirical. People used the terms 'water' and 'gold' long before they knew anything about molecules, atoms, and electrons. It was surely a discovery that no amount of reflection could have provided that the composition of water is H_2O, or that the atomic number of gold is 79. Hence, the *a posteriority* of such statements should not be in doubt.[8]

---

[7]Kripke, *Naming and Necessity,* p. 113.

[8]A caveat: One line of thought against the necessary *a posteriori* would maintain that insofar as we are convinced that these statements are indeed necessary, we need to reconsider whether they are indeed as empirical as they seem, that anyone who sincerely denies that no possible stuff could be water without being H_2O has adopted a new use of (meaning for) 'water', on which it is analytic that water is H_2O. I shall not pursue this line, though it has a certain plausibility. It is my hope, however, that the account that I shall offer will show conventionalists that they do not need to find ways of denying the necessary *a posteriori* in order to maintain their

What of their necessity? Here, as with any claim to necessity, we are asked to try to come up with a possible situation in which something was water without being H_2O, or gold while not having atomic number 79. Of course, since both of these facts are empirical, we can certainly imagine having discovered that water and gold had different deep structures. However, unless we are to beg the question against the very possibility of the necessary *a posteriori*, we cannot take this as establishing the relevant possibility.[9] We need to see whether we can come up with the relevant sort of situation while supposing (or 'in the knowledge') that water *is*, in fact, H_2O, and that gold does, in fact, have atomic number 79. And this, it is claimed, is something we cannot do. We reviewed Putnam's example of Twin Earth's XYZ, about which there is much agreement with Putnam that XYZ is not water. But it certainly seems that if anything could be water while not being composed of H_2O, it would be XYZ. This makes it plausible that water is necessarily H2O. Kripke gives a similar argument concerning gold.[10]

While it is not completely clear what accounts for these intuitions, they are fairly widespread.[11] And this makes a case for the necessity *a posteriori* of statements of substances' deep structures, and perhaps similarly for other properties.

This discussion is not meant to be exhaustive, either of the possible sorts of necessary *a posteriori* truths, or of the grounds of their current acceptance. But I hope they give a sense of why it is largely agreed that there are such truths, or, at least, of why one cannot just brutely deny this.

---

conventionalism. For a discussion that anticipates and rejects this move, see Putnam, "The Meaning of 'Meaning'," pp. 235–38.

[9]To this end, Kripke distinguishes between 'mere' *epistemic* possibility and *metaphysical* possibility. See Kripke, *Naming and Necessity*, p. 103.

[10]Ibid., pp. 124–25.

[11]One possibility is that it is because we know that the deep structures of substances account for their overt properties, their interactions with other things, and the laws under which they are subsumed.

The challenge to conventionalism, or on behalf of realism, which such truths provide, should, I hope, also be clear. First, we cannot learn such truths simply by reflection. We need to look at the world. But why would we need to look at the world if it was not to discover something about the world? We learn gold's essence by studying gold, and not by reflection on the word 'gold'. So it is straightforward to think that what we have learned is that a certain stuff in the world has, quite independently of any of our thoughts on the matter, or our concepts, the modal property of necessarily having atomic number 79. In addition to having a certain color and being usable in rings, it has this modal property. Similarly, necessary *a posteriori* truths are synthetic, and so, like any other ordinary synthetic truths, would seem to be true because they correspond to the facts. Modal truths, then, if synthetic, must correspond to modal facts. One would need an argument to make it reasonable to suppose that we have anything to do with these facts. Realism about necessity is just the natural way to understand the necessary *a posteriori*. The challenge is as simple as that.

One further reason for thinking that this phenomenon refuted conventionalism would be to suppose that conventionalists, as such, are committed to the view that all necessary truths are analytic and *a priori*. This could come from thinking that this is just what the view *is*, or from thinking that it is the only form conventionalism can take. As I have suggested in the first chapter, this is not what conventionalism *is*.[12] The basic claim of the conventionalist is that it is our decisions and conventions that explain and are the source of

---

[12]If, for whatever reason, someone is wedded to this idea, I am happy to give him the name 'conventionalism' and stick with 'empiricism' or some other suitable invention. The position I shall be defending is certainly disjoint from realism and would be, I believe, acceptable to anyone who has ever been a conventionalist, and for the very reasons he is a conventionalist. So, while titles are unimportant, it seems silly not to consider my position conventionalist.

modality. And while the traditional form the view has taken equates necessity with analyticity, arguments would be needed to show that this is the only form the view could take. I will now show how there could be conventions that would give rise to necessary *a posteriori* truths and thus that conventionalists, as such, are committed neither to the equation of necessity with analyticity, nor thus to the rejection of the necessary *a posteriori*.

The Necessary *A Posteriori*, Conventionalist Style

As we noted above, it is part and parcel of the necessary *a posteriori* that the negations of such truths be epistemically possible. That is, for any such truth, we can imagine discovering, or having discovered, that it was not the case.[13] If we could not so imagine (seem to imagine), the truth would be *a priori*. Now, when a proposition is proposed as necessary *a posteriori*, it is of course supposed that it is true, and if it turns out that we are wrong, we will retract our modal claim. So, if historical research reveals that Margaret Truman was actually the daughter of a hospital cook and wound up with the

---

[13]There is some question as to whether we should say that the negations of necessary *a posteriori* truths are imaginable, or only apparently imaginable. If one wishes to maintain the principle that whatever is imaginable is possible, then one must deny that these negations are ever properly imagined. One will say then, for instance, that when we seem to imagine water that is not H_2O, or having discovered that it was not, what we are actually imagining is stuff quite like water, which is not H_2O, and this *is* possible (see Kripke, pp. 141–44). If, on the other hand, one wishes to maintain the principle that when we seem to imagine something, we do imagine it, then one would have to deny that whatever is imaginable is possible. Given the necessary *a posteriori*, one of these principles has to go. If we abandon the former, we will say that the negations of necessary *a posteriori* truths can be imagined; if we let go the latter, we will say that we can *seem* to imagine their negations. For present purposes, I will stick with the former formulation; all that matters at present is that we can at least seem to imagine the negations of necessary *a posteriori* truths. I discuss this matter further in chap. 4.

Trumans due to an administrative foul-up, we would no longer maintain, naturally, that she was necessarily a biological daughter of Bess Truman. Similarly, if we are considering the epistemically possible situation in which scientists discovered that water was in fact XYZ, we would not maintain that in such a case, water would have been necessarily H_2O. Thus, what we put forth as necessary *a posteriori* depends on what we believe to be true.

Returning now to the epistemically possible, consider the case in which we find out that Margaret Truman is indeed the daughter of a hospital cook. Presumably, in such a case, we would have just as much reason to maintain that she was essentially a biological daughter of this cook as we do to maintain that she is in fact essentially a daughter of Bess Truman. There is nothing special about Bess pertinent to the case beyond the fact that she is actually Margaret's mother. It seems that whoever Margaret's mother actually is, Margaret essentially has her as a mother.[14] Similarly, consider the case where scientists discover that the chemical composition of water is XYZ, rather than H_2O. There is nothing privileged about H_2O which makes it essential to water, beyond the fact that it is water's actual chemical structure.[15] So if water turned out to be XYZ, we would have as much reason to deny that Twin Earth H_2O was water, and to assert that

[14]This should not be surprising, given that Kripke defends the general principle that all material objects have whatever origins they actually have essentially (see especially p. 114, n. 56). For present simplicity, however, I will be focusing on the particular case.

[15]For sticklers to detail, it might be claimed that it is the fact that H_2O is the *explanatory* structure of water, or that it is what makes water subsumable under laws, or some such, which makes it the essence of water. If this is so, consider it as built into the text that not only is XYZ discovered to be the chemical structure of water, but that it is its deep explanatory feature, or what have you. In claiming that there is nothing privileged about H_2O, I merely mean that whatever the features of H_2O are which, in virtue of their actually obtaining, make us claim that anything that is not H_2O is not water, they are epistemically possible of other chemical structures as well.

water was necessarily XYZ, as we actually have to do the reverse.[16] Whatever the chemical structure (deep explanatory feature)[17] of water, water has it necessarily.

This seems to be true generally. For any necessary *a posteriori* truth, there will be epistemically possible situations in which, since the actual facts in those situations are different, what is necessary is different. What is claimed to be a necessary *a posteriori* attribute is so because it is the actual value of a parameter that is such that whatever takes that value is necessary, and in each case, there seem to be no barriers to a variety of epistemically possible such values. Put slightly differently, for each necessity *a posteriori*, we can abstract away from the particular predicate that is in fact necessary, to a statement form with a blank, and constraints upon how that blank is to be filled in, for instance, 'Water is ____ (deep explanatory feature)' or 'Margaret Truman's biological origin was ____', such that however it gets filled in, the resultant statement expresses a necessary truth. Just what the constraints are can be determined by looking at the sorts of considerations that make us assert the necessity in the actual case, and finding the class of 'relevant alternatives' that we would be equally justified in asserting to be necessary had they turned out to be actual (see note 17). We will arrive, then, for each such truth, at another truth 'behind' it, as it were, which encapsulates the statement-forms with blanks;

[16]Putnam implies this in "The Meaning of 'Meaning'," when he says that "in the sense in which it is used on Twin Earth, the sense of water$_{TE}$, what *we* call 'water' simply isn't water" (p. 224).

[17]There is actually a reason for preferring the parenthetical formulation (and that mentioned in note 15). Many advocates of the necessity of water's being H_2O would, I take it, revise their view if it turned out that chemical composition wasn't of as much explanatory importance as is thought, or if, say, there turned out to be a deeper level more fruitful for use in scientific explanations. The structure of water at this deeper level might then be claimed to be its essence. (Here I am indebted to Philip Kitcher.) Note, however, that epistemically, there would still be multiple structures possible, which is what matters to the text.

an example might be "Whatever is water's deepest explanatory feature, water has it necessarily." When empirical features are essential, it is because of the type of feature they instantiate.[18]

Now, not only is it true that we can generally abstract from the particular predicates involved in necessary *a posteriori* truths; we can abstract from the subjects as well.[19] That is, if we take such a truth, and find the property-type the token of which, whatever it turns out to be, is had necessarily (say, biological origin, in the case of Margaret Truman), we can then abstract from, or generalize from, the particular subject, to some more general type of subject, such that any subject of that type necessarily has whatever instance of the property-type it actually has. Thus, for instance, it is not just Margaret Truman who has her origin, whatever it is, necessarily; this is equally true of all biological individuals, or perhaps of all material objects (this, again, is Kripke's contention). Similarly, it is not only water that has its chemical structure (deep explanatory feature) necessarily; so do all chemical compounds, or (taking deep explanatory feature as the proper specification) perhaps all natural kinds. Thus, not only are the necessarily-had properties of some type such that whatever instance the subject has, it has necessarily, but also the

[18]Note that the same is true, though perhaps different wording would need to be used, for identities.

[19]Neither of these points about 'abstractability' need be insisted upon; I will make clear later how there could be necessary *a posteriori* truths that were 'singular' in that neither the subject nor predicate belonged to more general types, such that all truths of a certain sort involving these types would be necessary *a posteriori* truths. While I think such singular truths do not sit very well with realism, but are no problem for conventionalism, there should be no problem with my ignoring them for the moment; it is the realist, if anyone, who needs to insist on 'abstractability' in *principle*. At any rate, principled or not, the ability to abstract as described in the text does seem to hold generally for the familiar cases of the necessary *a posteriori*, and so provides for ease of exposition. I hope it will become clear, if it is not already, that no decks are being stacked.

subjects belong to types such that any subject of that type has necessarily whatever instance of the relevant property-type it actually has. Indeed, it is not far-fetched to suppose that what makes a subject belong to a certain kind is precisely the sort of property it has essentially. At any rate, it now seems that where we have necessary *a posteriori* truths (or at least, in the familiar cases), we will also have general principles that these truths instantiate, which specify both subjects and predicates by their types, and which indicate that any subject of type x necessarily has whatever property of type p that it actually has; as a first shot at the form of such principles, which I will call 'general principles of individuation', we might try: (x)(If x belongs to kind K, then if p is x's P-property, then it is necessary that x is p), where x ranges over any sort of subject (individuals, properties, kinds—in each particular case, I take it that one of these domains will need to be specified), and a P-property is a kind of property (for example, origin, microstructure), of which p is an instance (for example, daughter of Bess Truman, H_2O).[20] In any case, of course, the kind and the type of property will have to be coordinated, thus supporting our suggestion that these principles tell us what it *is* for something to be of a particular kind. The arguments that are supposed to support the necessity of particular *a posteriori* claims, if they are successful, equally establish general principles of this sort; indeed, we might suppose that it is these general principles which are, at some deeper level, actually

---

[20]Just to make clear how these particular cases go here, we have: (1) (x)(If x is a biological individual, then (if p is the biological origin of x, then it is necessary that x originated in p)), or colloquially, biological organisms have their biological origins necessarily, and

(2) (x)(If x is a chemical compound [natural kind], then (if p is x's chemical structure [deep explanatory feature], then it is necessary that x has p)), or colloquially again, chemical compounds (natural kinds) have their chemical microstructures (deep explanatory features) necessarily.

There are some technical questions about whether these formulations are quite right, that is, whether all substitutions will in fact give us necessary truths. I postpone this discussion until the next chapter.

being argued for.[21] So it should be agreed on all sides, then, that if the familiar examples of the necessary *a posteriori* are what they purport to be, then there are appropriately specifiable general principles of individuation that are true as well.

We are now in a position to see how the necessary *a posteriori* could be susceptible to a conventionalist account. Suppose that general principles of individuation are analytic.[22] That is, suppose that rather than being general claims that describe features of a mind-independent modal structure of reality, these principles are instead object-level formulations of conventions we have adopted concerning how we will describe things, particularly when we are speaking of nonactual, or

[21]This is fairly explicit in Kripke's discussions both of the necessity of identity (pp. 3, 97–105), and of the essentiality of origin (pp. 111–14); while instances are used as examples, Kripke is clearly arguing for the general principles, and it is hard to see how one *could* argue for the necessity of particular necessities *a posteriori* without at least being willing—if not primarily intending—to advocate some general principles. (Note that the same does not hold for analytic necessities, since there is no requirement that our words be defined systematically in groups.)

While there should be no problem with calling the principle of the necessity of identity a general principle of individuation (it's at any rate general and 'lies behind' particular necessary identities), it is worth pointing out that it fits into our general formula for general principles by taking kind K to be vacuous (or filled in by 'thing', or some such), and the P-property to be that of being identical to something. Because of the trivial satisfaction of the kind K condition, we might think of this as the most general principle of individuation; for if P-properties define what it is for something to be of their K-kinds, then as the P-property does not here need to be tailored to any particular sort of thing, other than, say, 'thing', we might think of this as telling us what it is for something to be, or at least, to be a thing.

[22]The suggestion that this could be the case appears in appendix 2 of Nathan Salmon's *Reference and Essence* (Princeton: Princeton University Press, 1981), and its importance for the metaphysical significance of the necessary *a posteriori* is nicely noted by Paul Coppock in his review of Salmon's book (*Journal of Philosophy* 81 (1984): 261–70). While neither of them pursue what might be said for or against the suggestion at any length, my guess is that Coppock would be more amenable to the arguments I present in chapter 4 on behalf of the claim. My views on these issues were worked out before I became aware of these references.

hypothetical, cases. This may seem slightly odd, given that the paradigm cases of conventions that philosophers typically use involve the introduction of particular terms, with particularly specified definitions, or meaning constraints, for instance, " 'Bachelor' means unmarried man."[23] However, it should be clear that this is not required and that there is no principled barrier to our having conventions of a more general, abstractly specifying sort. We could, for instance, introduce the term 'earlytaste' to apply to all and only meals, in any possible situation, that include a bowl of the first cereal ever actually eaten. It would then be analytic, a matter of convention, that whatever cereal was actually first eaten is necessarily a part of earlytaste.[24] So the mere fact that general principles of individuation are general, and so may not look like 'paradigmatic' analytic truths, does not show that they could not arise from convention.

So suppose, again, that they are conventional, that is, analytic. Then it will be a matter of convention, say, that if something is a chemical kind, then it has its chemical microstructure necessarily. Thus, if we can add the ostensibly nonmodal 'Water is a chemical kind' and 'The microstructure of water is (actually) H_2O', we will be able to derive that it is

---

[23]This is as good a time as any to say that I shall not have much to say about the nature of conventions, though I suppose them to arise from the coordinated intentions and decisions of the members of some community. For the best going account of convention, see David Lewis, *Convention* (Cambridge: Harvard University Press, 1969). For my purposes—challenging realism about necessity—one need not think of conventions as arising from some 'event' of group agreement: conventions can be implicit, and postulated when they are the best account of group behavior, or some truth. Thus, for instance, it should be clear that for what I need, the account Quine offers of logic in the last few pages of "Truth by Convention" in *The Ways of Paradox* (Cambridge: Harvard University Press, 1966) makes logic conventional, even if Quine does not wish to apply the term 'convention' there; on his account, logic is certainly not made true 'by the world', but by the way we talk and think.

[24]Compare Coppock on 'Socratoon', p. 270.

necessary that water is H_2O, and all the modal force of this conclusion will be derived from our general principle, which we are supposing to be analytic. Our necessary truth will be *a posteriori* because of the nature of our convention, which requires that it be supplemented by *a posteriori* matters of fact before yielding a particular necessary truth, specifying more precisely, or directly, what the essential features, or individuative criteria are, in any particular case. But the necessity to water of whatever is found out to be water's microstructure is given by convention, and is not something which is discovered. That water *is* H_2O is an empirical, worldly matter; that it is *necessarily* H_2O would result from our convention. The necessity here would be no deeper than the necessity that bachelors are unmarried, and the appearance that it was would result primarily from the fact that we would have a more complex sort of convention that specifies the parameters, rather than the values, for our linguistic behavior, leaving the values to be discovered. The general strategy, then, for the conventionalist's account of the necessary *a posteriori*, is to maintain that we have conventions that specify that *whatever takes a certain value* is to be necessary—that is, to constrain our cross-world identifications—but that leave it as an empirical matter just what it is that takes this value. Again, there seems to be nothing to prevent our having conventions of this sort, and if we did have them, they would give rise to necessary *a posteriori* truths, the necessity of which would be explained by the conventions, and not matters of independent modal fact. There is nothing, then, in conventionalism as such that rules out the possibility of necessary *a posteriori* truths—it just depends on what sort of conventions we have—and, thus, the mere fact of there being such truths does not establish the falsity of conventionalism. The issue becomes whether realists or conventionalists have a better account of necessary *a posteriori* truths.

Now, it might be thought that the case has not yet been properly made out that we indeed have a possible conventionalist explanation of, say, water's necessarily being H_2O. For instance, in the above discussion, I said that the two links needed between the general principle about chemical kinds, and the necessity of water's being H_2O, are 'ostensibly non-modal'. This is important, for if these links in fact have modal import, the claim that it is only the general principles that can ground the necessity of the conclusion comes under challenge.[25] And, indeed, modal import there is. Most obviously, by supposition, it is necessary that water is H_2O—indeed, it is necessary *a posteriori*. And it might also be plausibly claimed—perhaps it must—that necessarily, water is a chemical kind. More subtly, given the general principle that if something is a chemical kind, it has its chemical microstructure necessarily, it seems that water should count as a chemical kind only if it is such that it has its microstructure necessarily. So to claim that water is a chemical kind is to make a claim with significant modal import. And worse, if, as the conventionalist claims, there *is* no real necessity, then what we would achieve by having analytic general principles of the sort I have been discussing would not be necessary *a posteriori* truths, but terms that could not apply to anything. That is, if there is no real necessity, then there is nothing out in the world which is such that it has its microstructure necessarily and, thus, nothing that, according to our convention, counts as a chemical kind. According to the conventionalist, then, analytic general principles of individuation should not be necessity-producing, but vacuous.[26]

There are further worries, which I will get to presently. But even this much should make it clear that while we can see how a conventionalist account might go, it still needs to be established that something along these lines can be adequate

---

[25] I am indebted to Robert Stalnaker for bringing this worry to my attention.

[26] For this problem, I am indebted (if that's the appropriate way of putting it!) to Nathan Salmon.

to even be a competing account of the necessary *a posteriori*. I am half inclined to say that, given how clear and straightforward the basic outline is, and given that there is no reason why we can't have conventions that specify things as we like, that it is reasonable to assume that there must be some technically adequate way of working out this approach—a reasonableness that becomes all the stronger when we see the arguments (in chapter 4) in favor of conventionalism. However, I do not expect others to see things this way, and, anyway, it would certainly be better to confront the worries here and now. In the next chapter, then, I will attempt to respond to the above and other technical worries that might be raised about the adequacy of my suggested conventionalist approach to the necessary *a posteriori*.[27]

Before the reader turns the page, let me offer an invitation. The contents of the following chapter are placed where they are because they are the elaboration of the project of the present chapter, namely, showing that a conventionalist account of the necessary *a posteriori* is possible, and thus that acceptance of such modal truths does not commit one to realism about modality. However, the discussion quickly becomes rather involved and, I am sorry to report, quite lengthy. My sympathies are with the reader who first wants to see why we should be sympathetic to conventionalism before wading through the material of chapter 3, or with one who is simply willing, for the moment, to suppose that a conventionalist account is possible and is more interested in getting right to the heart of the conventionalist/realist dispute than in seeing in detail what he can already see basically well

---

[27]I hope it is clear that this defense of the *adequacy* of this approach is not supposed to be a defense of its *correctness*, but is a mere preliminary to that. I am merely trying to establish the *possibility* of a conventionalist account here, and if I succeed, it remains to be argued (and will be, in chapter 4) that this is the account we should accept. Readers who find the following account merely *implausible*, then, should save their objections for chapter 4, where what now may seem implausible will, I hope become as clear as day.

enough, how the conventionalist account goes. For such readers, then, my invitation is to skip ahead now to chapter 4, which concerns itself with the troubles with realism about necessity and the advantages of conventionalism. Having seen this material, such readers will, I hope, then be more ready, interested, or motivated to see in greater detail just how the conventionalist account works, which, again, is the project of the next chapter.

3 Is It Possible to Be a Modern-Day Conventionalist? or, Responding to Some Technical Worries

In CHAPTER 2, I outlined a basic conventionalist strategy for explaining how there can be necessary *a posteriori* truths without there being any real, mind-independent necessity. The modal aspect of such truths is to be explained in terms of our conventions, while their epistemic status is to be explained by the fact that these conventions specify what is to be necessary only generally, leaving it open for empirical inquiry to determine the more precise or particular specification of these conventionally set boundaries. While the basic idea is, I hope, clear and intuitive enough, the realist may claim that this conventionalist account cannot work: that, insofar as it is able to generate necessary *a posteriori* truths, the modal aspect of these truths cannot be explained simply in terms of our conventions, and insofar as we countenance only convention-based necessity, our method cannot generate necessary *a posteriori* truths. The former suggestion is raised by noting that, as formulated, the empirical premises that need to be added to our general individuative principles will themselves be necessary, so that it is not clear that the modal status of the conclusion rests only upon our convention. In addition, since these premises are empirical, they are themselves necessary *a posteriori*, and it is not clear that one has explained necessary *a posteriori* truths conventionally if such truths themselves figure in the explanation. The latter suggestion is raised by noting that, as formulated, it seems that the supposition that our general principles are analytic, combined with a denial of real necessity, prevents the generation of any particular necessary *a posteriori* truths, since terms governed by these principles could not have any application. If something is a chemical kind only if it has its chemical microstructure necessarily, and nothing has any of its features (really) necessarily, then there are no chemical kinds. So without helping ourselves to real, mind-independent necessity, our conventionalist account will not be able to generate any of the desired conclusions, or, alternatively, insofar as we can generate such conclusions, their modal aspect will not be susceptible to a conventionalist explanation, as the empiricist requires.

In this chapter, I try to explain why my account does not fall to such objections by elaborating a deeper structure for the conventions which I hope to use to explain the necessary *a posteriori*. No hidden appeal to real necessity is needed to explain the modal status of the truths these conventions (with the appropriate empirical input) can generate, and such truths *can* be generated. While I do not pretend that this discussion will be definitive, I hope to illustrate the greater resources available to the empiricist, and the broader metaphysical picture that goes along with the denial of real necessity. With this laid clear, we should be able to see that the conventionalist can indeed offer an account of necessary *a posteriori* truths, and that the issue needs to be battled out at the metaphysical level, by asking whether the realist or the conventionalist has the more adequate story.

The First Two Objections:
How Not to Presuppose Real Necessity

The general conventionalist strategy for explaining the necessary *a posteriori* I have outlined might be described as

one of dividing and conquering. We try to divide such necessary truths into components that account for their necessity
but are conventional, and components that are empirical but
contingent, and thus try to eliminate the apparent metaphysical punch of such truths. The first worry I noted at the end of
the last chapter suggests that the dividing has not been satisfactory, because the empirical contributors are not in fact
contingent. In explaining the necessary *a posteriori*, then, we
are making use of truths which are themselves necessary *a
posteriori*. And this is not just a feature of my particular case,
as we can easily see by noting that our general principles tell
us that, whatever feature of some given sort a thing has, it
has it necessarily. Since we need to determine empirically just
which feature this turns out to be, and it is already specified
that whatever it is, it will be necessary, this truth—which
needs to be empirical if the result is to be empirical—will be
itself necessary *a posteriori*. So the problem seems quite general. One might object that this is not very important, since we
are making no use of the *necessity* of this truth, but only of its
truth, and that it is indeed its necessity that is at present being
explained. But there is another responsive tack that should
prove more satisfying.

First, while I have been speaking of the suggestion that
general principles of individuation are true by convention, I
have proceeded by giving the conventionalist's story in the
material mode, speaking not of the conventions themselves,
but of the truths that are made analytic by them. The conventions, of course, are in the first instance rules governing the
use of terms, or kinds of terms, and I may have gotten myself
into some trouble by proceeding at the object level. So let me
take a step back, and look for the rules of use that could make
the general principles analytic.

The general formula we have reached so far is: (x)(If x
belongs to kind K, then (If p is x's P-property, then it is
necessary that x is p)). A first stab at the linguistic, or 'formal
mode' presentation for this might be: (1) If 'x' denotes some-

thing[1] of kind K, then if p is the P-property of the thing denoted by 'x', then 'x' applies to something in any possible situation only if it is (has) p. (This should be read as a schema.)

We would then proceed toward our necessary truth with (2) 'x' denotes something of kind K ('Water' denotes a chemical kind), (3) p is the P-property of the thing denoted by 'x' (H_2O is the chemical composition of the thing denoted by 'water'), and thus to (4) 'x' applies to something in any possible situation only if it is p ('Water' applies, in any possible situation, only to what is composed of H_2O), and thus, returning to the object language, we get (supposing 'p' to express p), that it is necessary that x is p (necessarily, water is H_2O). So long as we read 'the thing denoted by 'x'' nonrigidly, we seem to have avoided having our empirical contributors be themselves necessary. While, for colloquial purposes, we may go along speaking in the material mode, the real empirical import of, say, 'Water is H_2O' can be found in 'Most (enough) of the samples that we call 'water' are composed of H_2O'. And, the conventionalist might add, this provides an attractive gloss on the 'epistemological possibility' of the falsity of the necessary *a posteriori*, for the real import of 'We might have discovered that water was XYZ' can be given by 'We might have discovered that most (enough) of the samples we call 'water' were composed of XYZ', and this really is (metaphysically) possible.[2] Ascending to the formal mode, then, we are able to eliminate the

---

[1] If the necessity of deep structure applies to kinds only, and not their instances (e.g., if it is not true that particular instances of water are essentially H_2O, i.e., water), then the rules for the application of 'x', where the substituend is a general term, will cover only the denoted kinds. Clearly, the proper reading of 'something' and, in general, the formulation of the rules a conventionalist should invoke in his accounts, will depend on what it is that is being explained, i.e., what is deemed to be necessary.

[2] Of course, then it would have been the case that most of what we called 'water', in that nonactual situation, would not in fact have been water, and 'water' would have had a different referent. But that is of no concern here.

problem of having necessary *a posteriori* elements present in the conventionalist account of (or generation of) the necessary *a posteriori.*

This, of course, does not solve all our problems and, indeed leads directly into the second problem raised at the end of the last section. In the modified account, I have replaced '*x* is of kind *K*' with "'*x*' denotes something of kind *K*'. But I am still supposing that if something is of kind *K*, then it necessarily has its *P*-property, that if water is a chemical kind, it necessarily has its chemical microstructure. Thus, in order for '*x*' to denote something of kind *K*, its referent must be possessed of certain modal properties. And this, again, is not something the conventionalist can stomach. In order for the terms here to be nonvacuous, as they must be if we are to generate any necessary *a posteriori* truths, there needs, it seems, to be independent modal features of reality, and if there *are* no such features, as the conventionalist claims, then there will never be substituends for '*x*' for which it is true that "'*x*' denotes something of kind *K*', so that even if we had analytic general principles of this sort, they would just dangle, doing no work, as we could never satisfy the first antecedent. Put more curtly, the charge is that the conventionalist should think it just silly to have conventions of this sort.

The conventionalist should not be surprised by this. After all, if kinds are determined by their modal features, as they seem to be if the claims associated with the necessary *a posteriori* are correct, then the conventionalist knows he has to account for the presence of such kinds. There is nothing new or radical about such a move in the empiricist tradition; it dates back at least to Locke. Locke, as we saw at the end of chap. 1, after stating his case that the kinds (sorts) of which we speak are bounded merely by nominal essences, concludes that "the essences and species of things . . . [are] the workmanship of the understanding."[3] Since the boundaries determine the

---

[3]John Locke, *Essay Concerning Human Understanding*, bk. 3, chap. 6, sec. 12.

sorts, if we make the boundaries, we, in some sense, make the sorts. So this is a familiar position for the conventionalist to be in. That the objection should not be surprising, however, still leaves us with the question of what the conventionalist should say. Given the principle concerning chemical kinds, how can it be the case that 'water' denotes a chemical kind, unless it is something with independent modal extension?

The conventionalist's obvious first stab here is to claim that it is analytic that water is a chemical kind, that 'water' is introduced as a chemical-kind term. However, while this gets us that water is a chemical kind (modulo worries about analyticity), it just pushes back our above problem. 'How can anything be a chemical kind?' becomes 'How can anything be water?'; we are still left with the question of how any chemical-kind term can have a nonempty extension, given that, according to the conventionalist, there is nothing in the mind–independent world that has modal extension.

But all this is to skew what the conventionalist is claiming when he suggests that our principles of individuation here are analytic. Clearly, he is not saying that these conventions supply, in the ordinary way, criteria for the application of a term, or a kind of term; that is, given his modal skepticism, he is not suggesting that these rules tell us, at least, in the first instance, that these terms apply only to items in the world that have the requisite modal features, for then, of course, they would be devoid of application. What these conventions must be understood to say, then, is that supposing certain *actual* conditions to hold, we are constrained in our descriptions of counterfactuals in a certain way. It is not that, say, 'water' or 'chemical kind' is to apply only to items that have their microstructures essentially, but, rather, that such terms are determined to have some actual application, and we then cannot count anything, in any possible situation, as of the relevant kind if it does not have the same microstructure (instances of) this actual application has. The task, then, for the conventionalist is to say how this actual application is determined in some way that does not require antecedently given, modally extended items.

Surprisingly, the conventionalist can find some help here from causal accounts of reference. Causal accounts focus on ostension and the use of exemplars, maintaining that the application of a term is given not by analytically associated descriptions (the extension of the term being those things which satisfy the description), but rather, those items which stand at the end of the 'causal chain' leading to the use of a term—the individual, in the case of singular terms, or the kind instanced, in the case of kind terms. Now, while no conventionalist is going to fully embrace a causal theory, there is no reason why he cannot make similar use of exemplars. While our general conventions govern our modal talk and our descriptions of other possible worlds, we still, as noted, need something to determine the actual application of these terms before those general principles can kick in. And if we are going to get necessary *a posteriori* truths, this application cannot be determined by ordinary analytically given necessary and sufficient conditions. So some use of exemplars is a quite natural supplement to analytic general principles of individuation.[4]

But just how will this go? We cannot say that if most (or enough) of the instances to which we have applied (or, through which we have introduced)[5] a term are members of a natural kind, then we will use that term to pick out that kind in all possible situations, for, here again, we are requiring

[4] I will return to this idea in chap. 6, when discussing semantic matters more directly. See pp. 194–201.

[5] I enter this alternative so as to remain neutral on the issue of whether we should take reference to depend more importantly on 'baptisms', or term introductions, than on everyday use, and that larger class of cases in which we use a term.

antecedently given, modally extended items. But what if we simply focus on the conditions we plan to use to govern our modal talk? That is, any kind K, according to our principles, is going to be given by some P-property. So why can't our rules be understood as saying that whatever instance of the relevant P-property most (or enough) of the items to which we have applied (or through which we have introduced) our term have, nothing will count as falling under that term in any possible situation unless it has that instance of the P-property? A term, then, will be a K-kind term *not*, in the first instance, because it picks out a kind of type K, but because it is governed by a rule to the effect that the P-property definitive of the K-kind that is found in most (enough) of the things to which we apply (through which we introduced) the term, will govern our counterfactual use of that term. 'Water', then, for instance, would be a chemical-kind term if it is a rule for our use of 'water' that whatever chemical microstructure most (enough) of the instances to which we apply 'water' actually have, nothing in any possible situation will count as water if it does not have that microstructure. The realist may claim that for most (enough) of these instances to share a common microstructure just *is* for there to be a real chemical kind with real modal extension. But the conventionalist need not make such a supposition, and since we are concerned with how a conventionalist line should go here, we need not at present accept it. The conventionalist will agree that under the given conditions there is indeed a chemical kind denoted by our term, but this fact is posterior to, and explained by, our convention (plus nonmodally packed independent facts). What is key for the conventionalist is that there is no requirement here that he presuppose independent modal extension, and this is accomplished in our present formulation; the only empirical fact that needs to be 'plugged in' to the sort of convention he proposes is that enough of the instances to which a term is applied in fact share a common feature (for example, a particular microstructure), and this does not require that there be anything with independent modal extension.

Let us briefly review and make explicit how the present proposal solves our problem. Our conventions, as formulated, start with the condition 'If '*x*' denotes something of kind *K*'. But since, if anything is of kind *K*, it necessarily has its *P*-property, this condition could never be satisfied unless there were items in the world with independent modal extensions. The conventionalist, then, needs to replace this condition by 'If '*x*' is a *K*-term', and to spell out what this amounts to in such a way as to allow '*x*' to have application without requiring independently modally extended items. What should make something a *K*-term, then, should depend fundamentally on the sorts of intentions with which we use the term, that is, on the rules that govern this use. And the idea that comes to mind is that something is a *K*-term just in case we intend to use it in such a way that, whatever the *P*-property happens to be of most (enough) of the items to which we apply (by which we introduced) the term, we will not apply the term to anything in any possible situation unless it has that *P*-property. '*X*''s being a term of kind *K*, then, hinges not on its picking out an independently modally extended item (a kind), but on our using it with certain intentions, and its having application depends not on there being such a modally extended kind, but merely upon there being enough actual *P*-similarity among the things we call by the term. The general conventionalist account of the situation then proceeds along the lines we have already discussed, with the fact that nothing counts as water in any possible world if it is not H_2O amounting not to there being in the mind–independent world some substance with a real essence consisting of a certain microstructure, but simply to there being enough actual similarity, at the level of microstructure, among the items we call 'water', to require us, given our rules for the use of 'water', not to count anything as water if it does not have that microstructure.

A Problem for Individual Essences?
A Brief Closer Look at Empiricist Metaphysics

But now another worry arises. While this account may work when general or kind terms are the subjects of our necessary truths, can it work for singular subjects as well, for truths like 'Necessarily, Plato is human' or 'Necessarily, Margaret Truman is a biological daughter of Bess Truman'? This looks problematic given the view just outlined, for while we can avoid direct talk about the referent, and the microstructure of the referent, of a kind term, in favor of talk about the structure of instances to which we apply the term, this seems not to be available for singular terms. We have only the referent itself, and so seem to need to talk about *its* origin, or kind-membership. And since, by hypothesis, this is necessary, whatever it is, our empirical fact will need to itself be necessary. We are confronted anew with the problem of how to get actual application conditions for singular terms that are not themselves modally packed.

Our first step, of course, will be to suggest that singular terms, primarily names, are introduced as terms of certain types, which can be discerned from the sort of counterfactual claims we are willing to make using the terms. If we think that whatever natural kind Plato belongs to, he belongs to necessarily, we might consider 'Plato' a 'natural kind name'. If we think that all material objects are such that they necessarily have their origins, we might have a class of 'material object names'. We shall then want to say what makes a name a 'natural kind' or 'material object' name in terms of the rules for the use of the name governing our counterfactual discourse, say, "'N' is a natural kind name just in case we intend to use 'N' in such a way that whatever kind-membership the thing we call 'N' actually has, 'N' applies to something in any counterfactual situation only if it belongs to that kind." And here our problem arises, for if we think it generally true that things belong to their kinds necessarily, then the thing we call 'N' will belong to a kind only if it satisfies a certain modal condition. We can generate our necessary truth only if there is already a necessary truth independent of our convention.

The simplest way around this would be to deny the general principle: it is not the case that all kind-members have their kind-memberships essentially. While Plato is essentially human, perhaps Lawrence Talbot is only contingently so. Identifying a thing's kind-membership, then, would require no modal commitments, and natural kind names could generate necessary truths in just the fashion of, say, 'hair-color' names, where our rule constrained our application of a name to an item according to hair color. While we could then get the *a posteriori* 'Errol Flynn (understood as a hair-color name) is necessarily red-haired', we would not require anything modal—only that the item prompting our use of 'Errol Flynn' had red hair. Similarly, we could then say that the item prompting our use of 'Plato' was human, without requiring antecedent modal commitment.

The drawback here is that we would need to deny, for any type of property that figured in a necessary *a posteriori* truth with a singular subject, that the property was such that it was had necessarily when had at all. And this looks like an unpromising commitment, particularly when we turn to the principle of the essentiality of origin. For insofar as this principle is plausible at all, it would seem to work for anything that has an origin. Thus, when we say that the object we call 'Margaret Truman' originated, in part, in a particular egg of Bess Truman's, we are appealing to something that must be necessary in order to be true. So we again have our problem. What empirical condition could we build into our linguistic rules that would get us a thing's origin as necessary, but that would not require actually determining what a thing's origin was?

It could be useful to think about the diversity of origins. Biological organisms have biological origins; artifacts are made by some artisan or machine out of certain materials according to certain plans; molecules and particles arise out of chemical or physical processes, and so on. Now, if everything has its origin essentially, it might be thought that there would be no need for our terms to be 'material object' terms, or any sort of term, in order to have true necessary statements in our language. I point to a chair, call it 'Ralph', and it will then be necessary that Ralph originated in a certain hunk of wood. But is this so? Let us suppose, for simplicity, that Ralph has undergone significant modification over the years—the legs, say, have all been replaced. We have then, colocated with Ralph, an organized collection of wood, the origin of which is not Ralph's origin—not all of the wood came from Ralph's original block or planks.[6] This is not to say that the origin of this collection of wood is not essential to it—only that its origin is not Ralph's. And so, of course, Ralph's origin is not essential to this collection of wood. Now we perform our ostension: 'I name this Ralph'. Is the sentence 'Ralph originated in wood W' now necessary in our language? Well, only if 'Ralph' picks out a chair, rather than a collection of wood. And this, it seems, cannot be just a matter of pure ostension—we must, at least tacitly, mean to be talking about the chair. So if our sentence is to express a necessary truth, 'Ralph' must be introduced as a chair name.

What is it to introduce 'Ralph' as a chair name? We might think it unproblematic to just say 'We mean it to pick out the chair'. But if being a chair is in part to have certain identity conditions, to be capable of certain, but not other, sorts of change, to have certain possibilities, and the like, the conventionalist cannot allow this. And, of course, this *is* required of something to be a chair, in the relevant sense. For if being a chair requires only satisfaction of certain actual conditions,

---

[6]One could think of collections of wood here either as sets of pieces of wood or only as organized collections, perhaps requiring some sort of physical unity or spatial continuity. Depending on how one took 'collection' here, one would get different origins. On either reading though, in our case, the origin will differ from that of the chair.

then our collection of wood is as much a chair as Ralph, and intending to pick out the chair will not get us Ralph, rather than the collection, as our referent.[7] But we are now familiar with the sorts of resource to which the conventionalist has recourse. To introduce 'Ralph' as a chair name is not to intend to pick out something with mind-independent modal features (as this would cause vacuity), but rather, it is to intend to use 'Ralph' in such a way that nothing counts as Ralph unless it can be tied to the thing to which we are pointing in accordance with our identity conditions for chairs.[8] And this will commit us, in part, to not calling anything 'Ralph' that does not have the requisite origin.[9]

Does this provide us with a better way, from the conventionalist's point of view, of spelling out the requisite origin? Well, we cannot of course just fall back to saying that something has to have Ralph's origin. But we have already seen that there is something important packed into the notion of 'requisite' here—the origin in question must be a chair origin. It is not that we just point and the thing at which we point has a certain origin: there are too many things at which to point that have different origins. In introducing a name as of a certain sort, we implicitly determine that the origin of the thing about which we are talking be the origin for that kind of thing. And Ralph's origin is not, in the first instance,

---

[7]This is not to say that there is not a perfectly good sense in which the collection of wood *is* a chair, but only that this can't be the sense of 'chair' in which we mean to pick out a chair in our use of 'Ralph'.

[8]Note that this does not trivially require that Ralph always and everywhere be a chair. This will depend on what the identity conditions for chairs are.

[9]Thus, it will not, in general, be sufficient to introduce a name as a 'material object' name, as this may be insufficient to distinguish potential referents with different origins. Of course, 'Ralph' will be a material object name, by being a chair name, and we may still say that the essentiality of origin stems from a general principle about material objects (or material object names), and in any particular case, from the name being a material object name. But something more is needed to determine an *actual* origin.

'the origin of that chair'; rather, it is the chair-origin to which we can trace back that to which we are ostending.[10] The reason, then, that we can say that Ralph originated in wood W, and so did originate essentially, is because we are using 'Ralph' as a chair term. In doing so, we are not merely intending 'Ralph' to pick out something with mind-independent modally packed identity conditions—a chair—but rather we intend to constrain our (actual and) counterfactual use of 'Ralph' in certain ways: we determine analytically, at some level of generality, what the identity conditions are for 'Ralph,' and this includes what sort of beginnings Ralph could have. There is then, no chair, appropriately understood, to which we are pointing when we introduce 'Ralph'—there is, as I like to say, 'stuff'.[11] And approaching

---

[10]One needs to be careful here. There is some suggestion that if we are ostending a chair with the relevant intention, still the object of our ostension had not only a chair origin, but, say, a 'collection-of-wood' origin as well, which may be different from the chair origin. We certainly do not want to be committed to a thing's having potentially contradictory origins. However, this is not what is being suggested. It is not that there is some object that is a chair, a collection of wood, and so on, but none of them essentially, and with only one real origin (this might even contradict the nonessentiality claim—find the real origin, and you'll know what kind of thing you're dealing with). We need to say that there is a chair, and a collection of wood, and so on, and that these are different things with (perhaps) different origins. However, we might say that metaphysically speaking, or 'considering the world mind-independently', what we are pointing at is in the first instance a lump or bunch of stuff, with no 'built-in' identity conditions or modal features, so that we cannot even clearly speak of some *thing* to which we are pointing. However, we can point in the relevant direction, and if we do so with 'chairish' intentions, we can then trace back to see when we first encounter chairishness, and consider that the origin of the chair. We can point in the same direction, with different intentions, and find different origins. However, given that we consider an object to begin at its origin, we cannot and need not say that there is a single object of ostension with different origins. What we have done is rather to carve up what is in some sense a single portion of the world into two overlapping but distinct objects, by focusing on different features.

[11]The appeal to stuff may seem peculiar to some, though I hope it does not. It is motivated, for the conventionalist, by his claim that, since there is

this stuff with a chair term, we can then determine an origin for Ralph by seeing, roughly, when this stuff started to be 'chairish.' But because there is no chair, strictly speaking, independently of our identity conditions, there is also no chair origin that is so independent: there is only a time when some stuff became organized in a certain way. And so to specify that Ralph will have his origin necessarily will not require appeal to some mind-independent fact of modal import.

To put this in the terms we have been using, the derivation of Ralph's essentially coming from wood W may go like this: If 'N' is a singular K-term (a K-name), and O is the K-origin to which the stuff through which we introduced 'N' is traceable, then 'N' applies to something in any possible situation only if it originates in O in that situation. For 'N' to *be* such a K-term is, in part, for it to be used with the intention of constraining one's counterfactual talk in this way, as well as other ways determined by the general principles associated with 'K' talk (for instance, concerning the application of a term to objects at different times). Since 'Ralph' is a chair term, and wood W is the chair origin for the stuff through

---

no mind-independent modality, there are then no objects with such mind-independent modal features. But since, in answering 'What is X?' type questions, we give answers that *do*, apparently, pick out objects according to what they are *essentially*, as of a type with *these* individuating conditions, then when saying what 'mind-independent' features of the world we are ostending, say, when we point and introduce 'Ralph', we cannot answer in any way that could be the value of 'x' in such a 'What is X?' question. (Of course, when we are not concerned with these technical problems, we can just say 'a chair'—but that is because we are speaking in a language with all the individuative principles in place.) Since any relevant predicate threatens to carry modal import, I think the conventionalist should, and should be happy to, say that what is primitively ostended is 'stuff', stuff *looking*, of course, just as the world looks, but devoid of modal properties, identity conditions, and all that imports. For a slogan, one might say that stuff is preobjectual. But be clear that there is nothing mysterious going on here— this is just elaboration of the rejection of real necessity. See chap. 1, pp. 19–24 and pp. 56–57 below.

which we introduced 'Ralph', nothing counts as Ralph that does not originate in wood *W*. Since we do not need to say, in our conditions, that anything had some actual origin— since to call something a 'chair-origin' is just to say when some stuff became 'chairish' (that is, came to have the actual conditions sufficient for saying that it is a chair [where 'is a chair' is read weakly, see note 11]), and one need not be committed to the necessity of this stuff's ever being 'chairish', or having become so in this way—we need make no appeal to anything that is necessary in the empirical conditions that give rise to our necessary truth. Our problem is handled by talking about 'stuff' instead of the proper referents of the names,[12] and so by not needing to talk about actual origins, but only contingent changes in the stuff.

Generally, then, we ought to be able to generate our necessary truths with singular subjects by appealing to the sorts of names we intend to use, the conventions governing names of that sort, and formulating our conventions to work from actual but modally innocuous features of the 'stuff' through which we introduce the names, rather than modally packed features of the referents of the names. As always, there will be nothing wrong with saying, for instance, that if something is human, it is necessarily human. This will just not be the generating principle at the deepest level of analysis.

This may seem far out of the way for the conventionalist to go to try to account for singular modal truths—being an empiricist about necessity carries some metaphysical baggage, even if only of a negative sort. Two replies are appropriate here. First, we need only go this far if we think there *are* necessary *a posteriori* truths with singular terms as subjects—perhaps some will dig in their heels here. Second,

---

[12]Again, while what we 'primitively ostend' is stuff, the stuff is not the referent of our term: the referent of 'Ralph' is a chair, an object of a certain sort, while the stuff is not. If one wants another slogan, objects of various sorts are what we articulate the stuff of the world into.

however, the move is neither that out of the way, nor un-motivated independently. For we have already seen, and seen this as a point at least as old as Locke, that at the level of kinds, the empiricist must be some sort of 'constructivist', if one likes. That is, if kinds are determined by their essential features, their boundaries, and according to the conven-tionalist there is nothing in the mind-independent world to carry this modal weight, then as we make the essences, we to that extent make the kinds. All I have suggested in the above is that we must recognize the same for individuals. If what it is to be an individual of a certain sort is to have certain features not only actually, but essentially, then the conven-tionalist has all the same reason to think that if there are any such individuals, they must also not be 'fully independent', but should arise out of our individuative practice, which is our way of articulating the world. This may still seem, for some, too stiff a price to pay. But I fail to see why this move should be more troublesome at the level of particulars rather than kinds, as it is motivated by precisely the same concerns; and, of course, I do not think that it *is* especially worrisome at the level of kinds. And if the only difference between ordinary objects and stuff resides in (or is a consequence of) their modal and individuative differences, then I do not see how any appeal to the 'strangeness' of stuff, as opposed to individuals, can be thought to carry any weight indepen-dently of dealing directly with the issue at hand, that of real-ism about modality. Stuff is no stranger than conventional-ism on this issue, and while the superiority of conventional-ism, of course, still needs to be argued for, I take it that the position is far from strange.[13]

---

[13]Indeed, chap. 1 was largely inspired by the collective opinion of others that what needs to be supported is the claim that anyone of interest *is*, actually, a realist in the sense I have discussed (although none of these others actually doubted that this is, in fact, the—or at least, a—quite prevalent position). I might add here that for those who actually suspect this, this book may be read as an attempt to spell out in some detail how

A minor caveat: As we have been spelling things out, the conventionalist is committed to the analyticity of true statements of the form 'x is of kind K', since we introduce our terms and names as of a certain sort. But it will be objected that instances of water, for instance, might have turned out not to have any similarity at the level of microstructure, so that it must be synthetic that water is a chemical kind. The conventionalist's response to this, oddly enough, can be extracted from a remark of Putnam's. Putnam mentions that in our 'ostensive definitions', there is a 'presupposition' to the effect that there is some deep similarity among the items that we have used to introduce our term, and that if this presupposition is false, we then revert to 'fall-back' conditions to determine the extensions of our terms, with these presumably given by our epistemic conditions for identifying items to call by our term.[14] The conventionalist too can adopt this strategy, maintaining that when we introduce a term as, say, a chemical kind term, we are saying that if there is a similarity at the level of chemical microstructure among the items to which we apply the term, then the term applies to items in counterfactual situations only if they have this microstructure. This conditionalization makes it, in a rather austere sort of way, synthetic that water is a chemical kind. But, it should be clear, this syntheticity is of no concern to the conventionalist, as the slightly modified version of the convention is still responsible for the modal status of the resulting necessary *a posteriori* truths.[15]

---

the conventionalist story should go for the necessary *a posteriori*, and for our thinking about individuation, objects, and reference; the present issue is presumably one that, even if we all are conventionalists, has not been much in the spotlight in connection with our thinking about these modal matters.

[14]Putnam, "The Meaning of 'Meaning'," pp. 225, 241.

[15]From a slightly different direction, the worry can be raised that it might turn out that the deep structural similarity shared by the items we call 'water' might not be chemical. This is further motivation for thinking

A Note on the Need for General Principles

We can also note, at this point, that the conventionalist need not suppose that all of our 'empirical-necessity-generating' conventions are general. We have been supposing, because it is so plausible, that there are general principles of individuation, and have thus had the conventionalist maintaining that we have rules governing kinds of terms (for example, natural kind terms), and that particular terms get introduced as instances of these. However, there is no requirement in principle, for the conventionalist, that this be so. We could, for instance, have intended to use 'water' in such a way that our counterfactual talk be guided by the common deep structure, if any, of the items we call 'water', without having any such conventions regarding other terms, even where we suspected deep structural similarity. In that case, it would be silly, or at least pointless, to say that 'water' was a chemical (natural) kind term, since there would be no other terms with which we were grouping it. The conventionalist would then say not that there was an analytic *general* principle of individuation behind the necessity of water's

---

that our general principles for kinds are pitched at the level of natural kinds rather than their more particular instances. The conventionalist should accordingly say that our terms are introduced as *natural* kind terms, with the condition being that whatever deepest explanatory feature, if any, is found among our samples, this is to guide our counterfactual talk, and if there is no such feature, all our talk is to be governed by fall-back criteria. Further modifications would be needed to account for cases like 'phlogiston', but there is no reason to think this could not be accommodated; the issue of when we determine terms to be vacuous is a problem for everybody, and the conventionalist can incorporate whatever the best account is into his constraints.

Note also that if we need to fall back on our fall-back conditions, it will then be peculiar to say that our term is a K-kind term. For technical perspicuity, then, we should say that our intentions make something a *potential* K-kind term, and reformulate our principles accordingly. (For simplicity, however, I will not do so.)

being H_2O, but would just describe the particular convention, perhaps calling it an 'individuating-feature specifying' convention.[16] Similarly, though it might be to no purpose, there is nothing to keep us from having conventions that are also not general from the point of view of the individuating feature. For instance, we need not have introduced 'water' so as to count *any* deep structural similarity as necessary—we could have just said 'If it turns out that most of the items we call 'water' are composed of H_2O, then nothing in any situation counts as water if it is not H_2O; otherwise, revert to fallback conditions'. Such a convention would be a bit bizarre, but we could do it, and it would generate the necessary *a posteriori* 'Water is H_2O' just as well as our other conventions would, with the modality again clearly coming out of the convention.[17] Thus, in offering explanations of the necessary *a posteriori*, the conventionalist is not committed in principle to supposing that, for instance, there are analytic general principles of individuation behind all such truths; he has only to provide some convention adequate for generating each truth, and their possible forms are varied (though the general idea is the same in each case).[18] Our proceeding along the lines of an explanation in terms of analytic general principles of individuation, then, is informed by the plausibility of it *in fact* being the case that necessary *a posteriori* truths run in packs, that they are not singular, to be explained by quite particular conventions, but in fact have more general conventions governing kinds of terms behind them. But in general,

---

[16]For simplicity and plausibility, though, I will continue to speak of general principles of individuation.

[17]Here, the *a posterioricity* of 'Water is H_2O' would be of the same austere sort as the syntheticity of 'Water is a natural kind' mentioned above.

[18]This should make good my earlier claim that no questions were being begged in favor of conventionalism by supposing that there are, in fact, true general principles of individuation. The plausibility of the supposition merely provided us with a natural starting point for presenting the conventionalist's general strategy.

just what the conventionalist needs to and should claim to be analytic will depend on what it is in fact plausible to suppose is necessary *a posteriori*—for he is trying to explain such truths, and explanations need to be tailored to what it is that is being explained.

We have, then, I hope, dealt with the two objections to the possibility of our conventionalist explanation which were raised at the end of chap. 2. However, there are two more worries that we need to address. The first maintains that our conventionalist explanation generates too many necessary truths, the second that it generates too few. I turn to these in the next section.

Two More Worries: Rigid Designation and Modality *De Re*

Even with our more linguistic formulation of the conventions to which one might appeal in explaining the necessary *a posteriori*, it may be thought that they are not adequate to their task. On the one hand, it seems that too many truths come out as necessary, because there are not enough constraints on what terms we may use to express our *P*-property. In my account, I noted only parenthetically that if we are to get as a statement in our object language: 'It is necessary that *x* is *p*', '*p*' must pick out the relevant *P*-property. But there are many ways in which such properties may be picked out, and not all of these properly figure in necessary truths. Thus, the description 'the chemical structure whose formula most commonly appears in philosophy articles' may well pick out H_2O, but we would not want to endorse the statement 'Water has the chemical structure whose formula most commonly appears in philosophy articles' as expressing a necessary truth (at least, on its ordinary reading). But this seems to fall out of our proposed conventions as straightforwardly as the necessity of 'Water is H_2O'. So our principles are too loose.

On the other hand, it is not clear how our principles can generate another class of central modalities, namely, modalities *de re*. And this is critical, since it might be thought that it is really these sorts of truths that provide the strongest argument for realism about modality. For *de re* modalities are ordinarily understood as attaching to their objects, independently of how they are described, and they warrant existential generalization. If our principles cannot be formulated so as to generate such modal truths, then, they are too stringent or, at least, do not cover the full range of realist-supporting modal phenomena. If we are to have a possible conventionalist account, then, we must be able to get our principles, or some others, to explain *de re* modal truths.[19]

Do Our Principles Generate Too Many Necessary Truths?

First to the looseness of my proposed explanation. It does not seem to me that it is in fact the case that the conventions we have formulated generate as necessary, for instance, that water has the microstructure most commonly mentioned in philosophy articles. After all, the conventions tell us that 'water' applies to an object in a possible world only if that object has the deep feature enough of the (relevant) items we actually call 'water' have. 'Water has the microstructure most commonly mentioned in philosophy articles' will be true in all possible worlds, then, just in case the predicate ('has the

[19]It would certainly not be out of place for a conventionalist who had accounted for necessary *a posteriori* truths to maintain that there were, in fact, no true *de re* modal ascriptions, and to suggest, perhaps, that the appearance that there are stems just from a looseness of speech, or from supposing that if some modal truth were *a posteriori*, then it had to be because of the way the world is, so that there would be no need to confine our formulations of these truths to the *de dicto*. But, of course, it would be more satisfying not to have to do this, and to provide an account, which is what I shall try to do; I wish only to suggest the somewhat attenuated force of this worry, at least if the rest of my account is satisfactory.

microstructure . . .') applies to an object in any possible world only if it has the deep feature enough of the items we actually call 'water' have. And this, presumably, is not the case. Generally, the only sentences that our conventions tell us will express necessary truths are those in which the predicate applies only to items, in any possible situation, that have the relevant *P*-property. The appearance, then, that our conventions are too loose actually stems from the casualness with which I earlier tried to generate a particular necessary *a posteriori* truth, that is, from my parenthetical "'*p*' denotes *p*'. If we pay proper attention to the convention, we can generate object-level necessities only by restricting our predicates to terms that apply only to objects, in any possible situation, that have the *P*-property by which the application of the *K*-term is restricted.[20]

This restriction on the generation of necessary *a posteriori* truths might be formulated this way: If '*x*' is a *K*-kind term, then '*x* is *p*' is necessary just in case '*p*' rigidly designates the *P*-property constraining the application of '*x*'. These necessary truths will be *a posteriori* when, as will generally be the case, it is an empirical matter just what *P*-property in particular does restrict the application of the *K*-term, that is, what

[20]Note that while we formulated our conventions as beginning with 'if '*x*' denotes something of kind *K*', we were subject to what really was an objection of the type we have been discussing, only with respect to the subject term. Then, unless we constrained the substitutions for '*x*' somehow, we would get, for instance, that it is necessary that King Midas's favorite element has atomic number 79. (I am indebted for the example to Nathan Salmon.) However, by moving over to 'if '*x*' is a *K*-kind term', we in effect build in the relevant constraints; as ordinarily used, 'King Midas's favorite element' is not an element (natural kind) term, and thus cannot be substituted into our schema. If that description *is* used with the intentions that would make it an element (natural kind) expression, it can be substituted, and would generate a necessary truth—but on that reading, the truth *is* necessary. It might be worth bearing in mind for the discussion that follows that what we have in effect done with our reformulations is, without making any explicit modal commitments, determined that *K*-kind terms be rigid designators.

P-property is had by enough of the items we call (by which we introduced) '*x*'. Our problem, then, seems to be solved.

On Rigid Designation

But is it legitimate for the conventionalist to make use of the notion of rigid designation? The notion of rigid designation is, after all, part and parcel of the realist program in modal metaphysics. By using a term rigidly, we are supposed to be able to get determinate reference to some object or property and then study it—consider it in other possible worlds—without having already determined in a qualitative way what features an object must have in order to count as the object to which we have originally referred. This stands in contrast to the empiricist tradition where terms are introduced by definitions, or definite descriptions, so that in order for an object in another possible world to be picked out by a term, it must satisfy this description, so that on the object level, if our term is '*x*' and our definition '*F*', we already know that something is *x* just in case it is *F*. If one likes, such definitions tells us wherein cross-world identity consists, whereas if we can introduce terms as rigid designators, without built-in qualitative constraints, we can discover wherein such identity consists. And this discovery, of course, is supposed to be of something that antedated our thought and talk. A rigid designator, then, is a term that applies to the same item in all of our descriptions of possible worlds, and for a term to be rigid, then, it seems that there must be real transworld identity prior to our use of the term as rigid. To make use of the notion of rigid designation, then, seems to be to buy into independently existing, modally extended entities and is thus not something to which the conventionalist can help himself.

Now, there is no doubt that, as ordinarily understood, rigidity is as much a metaphysical as a semantic notion, and one with metaphysical presuppositions. However, the conventionalist need not accept this ordinary understanding, and this in two ways. He may claim that there need be nothing especially metaphysical about the requirement for preexisting cross-world identity, or that the notion should be understood more purely semantically. I present these responses one at a time.

The first suggestion here is that in order to introduce a term as rigid—in order to intend to use it rigidly—it does need to be the case that cross-world identity is already in place. But this need not be because it is out there, determined by a mind-independent modal structure of reality; rather it could be because we already have general conventional principles for individuating items across worlds. We point to a fellow and say 'Let's call him 'Freddy''. We could explicitly introduce this rigidly, or it could be elicited from us by the question 'Could Freddy have failed to be Freddy?', with a negative answer showing that we are using the name rigidly.[21] Now, we ask whether Freddy could have been president, perhaps saying that he could have been. Now, does any of this require that in any deep sense, we must suppose that in the vicinity of our pointing, there is an item with mind-independent modal properties? Could we not have in place already a general convention governing our modal talk concerning human beings, or, more in keeping with our earlier discussion, for modal talk involving human being terms? We need not suppose that there is some modally extended entity out there waiting—rather, 'Freddy' is a human being (organism, material object) term, and the term applies to objects in other worlds that have (say) a certain origin. Since origins don't (metaphysically or semantically) rule out presidency, 'Freddy' could apply to something that was President.

But what of 'Freddy''s rigidity? Well, by having criteria of individuation for human beings, we are in a position to say

---

[21]See Kripke, *Naming and Necessity*, pp. 48–49.

what counts, or whether something can count, in another situation, as the same human being. We can thus introduce 'Freddy' as a term for 'this human being' (or as a human being term for 'what I am ostending') and say that 'Freddy' applies, in any situation, to what counts as this human being, given our criteria. In whatever sense we must have preexisting modally extended entities in order to introduce a term rigidly (or at least, rigidly and by ostension), we have it in this case, even though it is our convention that is doing all the modal work, that is, making it the case, 'prior' to our ostension, that what we ostend exists in other possible worlds. To use terms rigidly, then, it is not necessary that we make any deep metaphysical presuppositions.[22]

This is not that far from our second strategy, which is to understand the notion of rigidity as more purely semantic. Now, if 'x' is rigid, if 'x' actually denotes z, then for any item y in another possible world, if it is denoted by 'x', y must be identical to z. This suggests the picture that we get 'x' to pick out some z, intend to use it rigidly, and then when we talk counterfactually with 'x', it picks out the object(s), if any, in the relevant worlds, which are (independently) identical to z. But why can't it be the case that in introducing a term as

[22]One may harp on the fact that for our account to work, when we introduce a term as rigid, we must intend it as a K-term, for some suitable K, and that in fact we need not do this. When we point at Freddy, we can just give the name, without adding, say, 'human being'. But is this so? Surely, when we point at Freddy, there are a multitude of objects in the vicinity, including the collection of Freddy's present molecules. If 'Freddy' is to rigidly designate Freddy, and not these molecules, we must somehow intend the human being (material [continuent] object). Of course, this need not be explicit—it may be that in ordinary discourse, there are 'preferred' entities, such that when we ostend without further elaboration, it is clear what is meant (or, put conventionalistically, how the term is to be understood). Indeed, it should be obvious that this is in fact so. So this is not much of a worry. However, it does suggest that our familiar picture of rigid designators as terms that can just be ostensively introduced, with no conceptual content, may be importantly mistaken. I pick up this theme in chap. 6.

rigid—in intending to use it as rigid—we are rather *determining* which y's and z's are to count as cross-world identicals, along these lines: 'they are identical if they are both values of this term: 'x''?[23] Rather than the application of rigid terms being constrained by the prior facts about cross-world identity, the facts about cross-world identity are determined by our use of terms as rigid.

Now, to be sure, this requires that there be criteria of application for rigid terms other than: Whatever is identical to this. If transworld identity is not a matter of mind-independent modal fact, a term cannot be both rigid and purely ostensive (which is the double-duty [most] rigid designators are supposed to serve in most treatments). But the conventionalist of course neither needs nor desires to maintain that rigid designators—or anything else, for that matter—are purely ostensive. As a human being (material object) term, 'Freddy' *is* imbued with criteria of application which do not require prior determination, in other worlds, of

---

[23]We must be careful here if this is to cover the rigid use of definite descriptions. If one uses 'the president of the United States' rigidly to pick out a certain human being, certainly the idea is not to find the value of 'the president of the United States', ordinarily understood, in the actual world, and to identify him with the values in other worlds. However, if we are using this description rigidly for a human being, this is the wrong understanding, for we are then using the description as a human being term, and must look for the values of the expression in other worlds *so understood*, i.e., who, in these other worlds, comes from the relevant origin? We could use the description rigidly in another way, in accordance with the more straightforward reading, so as to indeed identify the (apparently) various values of the expression with its ordinary criteria of application; then 'the president of the United States' would rigidly designate not a human being, but a much more peculiar sort of entity, one that we would say, I take it, supervened on George Washington et al. Bizarre perhaps, but if there is nothing in principle wrong here, this shows again why a term cannot simply be introduced both rigidly and purely ostensively (see below). And if rigid designators do require descriptive content, as I am suggesting, they cannot serve the metaphysically important function for which the realist needs them.

which individual is *this* one.[24] In this way, the two lines of response I have suggested for the conventionalist come together. In understanding rigid designators as providing constraints on cross-world identifications, they are seen to require some descriptive content, as we saw provided in our first response above. In that first response, however, it was not made exactly clear why, even if we had rules for the application of a particular term in counterfactual descriptions, we had to think of the referents *given* this application as identical. I thus think that the conventionalist should advocate an account of rigid designation that makes use of both of these threads of thought, with rigid designators both determining our cross-world identifications (and thus determining what count as single items) *and* providing descriptively our criteria of individuation (even if only generally specified) for the objects of our reference.[25] The realist, of course, may stick with the more familiar and less complicated account, although I have tried to indicate along the way (see notes 22 and 23) why I think, at least partly independently of the modal matters at stake, something along the above lines is superior to the usual treatment of rigid designation.[26,27] My main purpose here has only been to show that the conven-

[24]I hope it is clear that this does not mean that we cannot use rigid designators to 'stipulate' possible worlds, in the way that Kripke rightly says we can and do. It merely means—as I take it is now familiar to anyone who thinks that some things are (really or nominally) essential—that not just anything can be stipulated.

[25]Nonrigid designators, on the other hand, do *not* (are not intended to) provide such criteria of individuation—they provide only the criteria of application in the world being described.

[26]For a very nice discussion of the connection between rigidity, in the metaphysical function it is supposed to serve, and 'direct' reference, see A. D. Smith, "Rigidity and Scope," *Mind* 93 (1984): 177–93.

[27]Note, though, that even on the conventionalist account, it remains true that rigid designators have the same reference in all possible worlds; the definition of 'rigid designator' is not at stake here, only its interpretation.

tionalist can make use of the notion of rigid designation without abandoning his position, and thus that we can in fact generate—or more particularly, restrict the generation of—conventionalist-style necessary *a posteriori* truths along the lines I have outlined. This, again, is not yet to argue *for* a conventionalist account, but only to show that such an account is possible.

Modality *De Re*

This brings us to our final worry, that concerning *de re* modality. Modal statements are typically distinguished as either *de dicto* or *de re*. A simple and familiar way of getting at the distinction is to note two readings of 'Necessarily, the number of planets is odd'. Formally, the two readings may be presented thus: (1) Necessarily $(\exists x)(x$ is the number of planets and x is odd) and $(2)(\exists x)(x$ is the number of planets and necessarily x is odd). The first statement says, roughly, that the sentence 'The number of planets is odd' is necessarily true—go to any possible world, count the planets, and you will get an odd number. This is the *de dicto* reading of the statement: some proposition is held to be true in all worlds; the modal operator applies to the *dictum*. In this case, the statement so understood is presumably false: the number of planets could have been eight. Statement (2) says that there is some number which is the number of planets, and this number—nine—is necessarily odd. This is the *de re* reading: some designated object is held to have a certain property in all worlds (or in all worlds in which it exists). In this case, the statement so understood is presumably true: nine *is* necessarily odd. There might have been eight planets, still, but this is of no consequence; 'is necessarily odd' is being applied to the number that actually numbers the planets, and the number of planets in other worlds is irrelevant to the evaluation of a statement with the logical form of (2).

The distinction between (1) and (2) is a scope distinction: in (1), the modal operator governs a quantified statement, while in (2), the modal operator occurs within the scope of an existential quantifier. And so it becomes tempting to see the *de re/de dicto* distinction as a scope distinction: in *de re* attributions, modal operators occur within the scope of quantifiers, while in *de dicto* attributions, they do not. However, not all statements are quantified. What should we do with 'Necessarily, Plato is human' (assuming, of course, that 'Plato' is not a disguised description)? One might think that it doesn't really make much sense to consider such a statement as falling under either category, since it is hard to see what could be the difference between saying that the proposition 'Plato is human' is necessary, and saying that Plato has the property of being necessarily human.[28] Nonetheless, one might argue for a *de re* reading of such singular statements, since they allow existential generalizations in which modal operators occur within the scope of the quantifier, as in 'Someone is necessarily human'. So we might say: A modal ascription is *de re* if (1) it is quantified and has a modal operator within the scope of the quantifier or (2) it is not quantified, but allows existential generalization to a statement of form (1), and it is *de dicto* otherwise.[29]

Now, I have no major beef with this way of drawing the distinction, but it does seem to me to miss the major point, and to get things backwards. Singular modal predications are *de re* on this account rather derivatively, because of their relation to quantified statements of a certain sort. But let us look back to our original case. What makes us say that a certain reading of 'Necessarily, the number of planets is even' is *de re* is not, in the first instance, that the operator and

[28]Although one could claim that the former, but not the latter, would be false in worlds in which Plato does not exist.

[29]I have obviously been ignoring statements involving multiple quantification; that there is no need to go into these further complexities should be soon apparent, as I opt for an alternative way of formulating the matter.

quantifier are related in a certain way, but that read in this way, the statement says, *of a certain number*, that it is necessarily odd. The important distinction is that between the necessity of a certain proposition or sentence (*de dicto*), and the necessity of a certain item's having a certain property (*de re*). *De re* attributions are modal predications. They are ascriptions of modal properties, and *de dicto* ascriptions are not. This is why *de re* ascriptions are referentially transparent, allow substitutability via Leibniz's Law, and allow existential generalization—this is true of anything with the logical form of a predication. This is similarly why *de dicto* ascriptions fail on all these counts—they are just not predications.

Now, quantified statements, even with modal operators falling within the scope of the quantifiers, are not predications, modal or otherwise. But their instances are modal predications. And such quantified statements are formed by the application of modal operators to predicates (or open sentences), thus forming modal predicates, and then quantifying. Thus we can see how quantified statements with internal modal operators involve modal predication, and why it is *because* of this that the quantifier occurs to the left of the operator. *De dicto* statements are not formed in this way; consequently, their instances will *not* be modal predications, but nonmodal ones.

Thus, I should like to say that *de re* modal ascriptions are those which involve modal predication, either by being modal predications, in the case of singular statements, or by having modal predications as instances, in the case of quantified statements. Otherwise, they are *de dicto*. Extensionally, we get the same results as on our earlier formulation in terms of scope, for the reasons just given. But here it is made explicit that what makes an ascription *de re* is that it ascribes modal properties to items, that we are concerned with some particular item and what is true of it in all (or some) possible situations. And it is because the scope distinction tracks this difference, at the level of quantified statements, that we can, or might be inclined to, draw the distinction as one of scope.[30]

So much for lengthy preliminaries. Now, the reason the distinction is important for us is that *de re* ascriptions, being predications, seem to involve us trivially in commitment to real modal properties if we think there are some true *de re* statements. For we are not just saying, as with *de dicto* statements, that if one description applies, so must another. Being real predications, and, as evidenced by the possibility of existential generalization, the applicability of the predicate does not depend on how the subject is described. It applies to the object itself. So if Plato is necessarily human, and this is a *de re* ascription, then Plato, quite independently of how he is picked out, has the property of being necessarily human. And one might even claim that the realist 'look' of the necessary *a posteriori* actually comes from this source: it is not in the first instance because such truths are *empirical* that they support realism about modality; rather, they are empirical because they involve real predication. The truth of *de re* ascriptions, if any there be, seems then to commit us to realism about modality. And so far, our efforts have been geared toward showing how there can be empirical modal truths, not toward how there can be true modal predications. Can the conventionalist story we have offered account for *de re* modal truths?

It is important to bear in mind that the distinction, despite the names involved, is one of logical form, not of metaphysics. To say that an ascription is *de re* is not to say that what makes it true, if anything, is some mind-independent feature of reality. It is only to say what sort of inferences it licenses, and to give the structure of what would make it

[30]The blame for the length of this opponentless tirade is my own; the praise for what is true in it should go to Robert Stalnaker. For an important and enlightening discussion of (complex) predicate formation, and the importance of distinguishing predications from other forms of assertion, see his "Complex Predicates," *The Monist* 60 (1977): 327–39.

true. As we've seen, a plausible-looking argument can be given that there are realist metaphysical requirements for the truth of *de re* ascriptions—it's just important to see that argument is *needed*.[31] What I shall now try to show is that the apparatus we have already discussed is itself adequate to the task of producing *de re* necessary truths and thus that, however realist 'looking' such truths may be, they do not in fact require real, mind-independent modal facts: there are no barriers to a conventionalist *de re*.

So far, we have not been concerned with the logical form of the necessary *a posteriori* statements we've been trying to provide a conventionalist framework for; we have been more focused on these necessary truths being empirical and synthetic. But do we have any reason to suppose that these truths could not be *de re*, that they could not have the form of modal predications? In a way, it is tempting to just say that these are our conventions, and we can give them any form that we want. However, we can be more informative.

What is it that marks off modal predications? Well, the simplest mark is that as we go from world to world in the evaluation of such statements, the only states of affairs that have a bearing on their truth are those that contain a single subject, that is, the subject relevant to the evaluation must be in all worlds the same. This is precisely because whether or not something has the property of being necessarily (possibly) *F* depends on whether, in all worlds in which it exists (some world), *it* is *F*. This contrasts with the evaluation of *de dicto* statements in that for the latter, whether some possible state of affairs is relevant to its truth does *not* depend on the identity of its objects. 'Necessarily, the president of the Unit-

---

[31]Of course, one could draw the (a) distinction between modal ascriptions that are made true by mind-independent modal features of reality and those made true by convention, and, with some claim, call the former *de re* and the latter *de dicto*. The distinction then *would* be one of metaphysics. For that very reason, though, one could then not establish that a modal truth was *de re* just by pointing to its logical form.

ed States is male', is falsified by a possible world state in which some woman is the president; it is of no relevance that this woman is not identical to the actual president. However, there is also a reading of the statement according to which this possible state of affairs does not render it false, and precisely because this woman is not identical to the actual president. This latter, of course, is the *de re* reading: it is a modal predication of a particular individual. So, perhaps not surprisingly, the truth of modal predications is tied up with the issue of transworld identity; in contrast with *de dicto* statements, the *de re* depends on whether in all (some) worlds, some particular entity—the same one in each case—satisfies a certain predicate.

Since it is always the same entity, in a *de re* statement, that is relevant to its evaluation, it is tempting to suggest that ordinary language modal ascriptions are *de re*, are predications, just in case the subject term of the statement is a rigid designator. If a term is rigid, it picks out the same entity in all possible worlds, and, thus, the truth of statements involving rigid designators will depend solely upon whether, in each (some) world, that thing has the property ascribed. And if some particular thing has some property in every world in which it exists, then (so long as we have vocabulary for the property) this will make true some necessary ascription *de re*. Conversely, since the truth of a modal predication depends on whether some entity has some property in all (some) worlds in which it exists, its being the same entity in each case would seem to make the subject term of such an ascription rigid. Thus, if the conventionalist account we offered is able to produce necessary *a posteriori* truths in which the subject term is a rigid designator, it is thereby able to produce true modal predications, that is, modal truths *de re*.

And, as we discussed at some length earlier, our conventionalist account is quite adequate to this task. Indeed, on our account, the use of terms in such a way as to provide for the possibility of their being the subjects of necessary *a posteriori* truths *makes* them rigid designators (pp. 64–68). This, we may recall, was because the conventions governing such use provide not only criteria for the application of these terms, but criteria of individuation for their referents. At any rate, since we have a conventionalist account of rigidity, and nothing to prevent rigid expressions from being the subjects of our produced necessities *a posteriori*, our conventionalist account can indeed produce modality *de re*.

Perhaps a slightly different tack could be more helpful. Look back to our account of necessary *a posteriori* truths involving singular subjects, and consider our generating 'Necessarily, Margaret Truman is a biological daughter of Bess Truman'. Is there any reason why we should not think that this has the logical form of a modal predication, that it is *de re*? If it is not, then it should be the case that some of the possible states of affairs which go toward the truth of this statement (or: some concomitant state descriptions licensed by the conventions governing the components of this statement) consist wholly of individuals other than Margaret Truman, that is, of someone who is not actually Margaret Truman, but who is Margaret Truman in that world, being there born of Bess Truman (or whoever is Bess there). It should also be compatible with this truth, if it is but *de dicto*, that there exists a world in which the entity there who is identical with (the entity that is) Margaret Truman here has an origin that does not biologically involve Bess Truman. Are these compatible with 'Necessarily, Margaret Truman is a biological daughter of Bess Truman' as we have derived it?

I think not. We will recall that our principles will produce necessary *a posteriori* truths only when the terms involved are used rigidly. If this were not a requirement, we would be able to derive the necessity of 'The woman whose name appears most often in this chapter is a biological daughter of Bess Truman', which, as we have seen, we cannot (unless the description is used rigidly). But if 'Margaret Truman' appears rigidly in our necessary *a posteriori* truth, then it cannot be the case that someone in another world could be identical with (the entity who is here) Margaret Truman without being Margaret Truman. And if she is Margaret Truman, then, as the principle says, she must there be a biological daughter of Bess Truman. Conversely, if some woman in another world originates without the help of Bess Truman, then she cannot be identical with the woman who is actually Margaret Truman, for if she were, she would be the value of 'Margaret Truman' in that world, thus falsifying 'Necessarily, Margaret Truman is a biological daughter of Bess Truman'. So the hypothesis that our principle as derived is compatible with the mere contingency of a Bess Truman origin for the woman who is Margaret Truman, is false. Similarly, we can see that any person in any world whose origin is part of the necessity of 'Margaret Truman biologically originated in Bess Truman' must not only be the semantic value of 'Margaret Truman' in that world but must indeed be identical to our Margaret Truman, that is, to the semantic value of 'Margaret Truman' in the actual world. This follows directly from the rigidity of 'Margaret Truman' as it figures in our generation of this necessary truth.

Thus, the telltale signs of a modal statement's being *de dicto* are lacking from our necessary *a posteriori* truths, and, indeed, all the features are there which make for true modal predications, that is, modal truths *de re*. The requirements of identity which seem to distinguish the *de re* from the *de dicto* are built into our scheme for the conventionalist explanation of the necessary *a posteriori*.

While I think this suffices, there may be some to whom it seems that some slight of hand must be going on. For after all, all that our conventions do is regulate our talk (thought), while the truth of modal predications seems precisely independent of how we describe a subject. They require that some object have some modal property, and this is just what the conventionalist denies. If there is no real modality, how can our talk imbue objects with such properties? How can

our conventions do more than make some sentence necessary? Something fishy must be going on if the convention-
ist is to get more than modality *de dicto.*

Of course, the primary response here is just to go through
the account again and to show that what this opponent says is
impossible can be done. However, difficulty may persist if
one does not see *how* it is being done, that is, what is wrong
with the above line of thought. And here, we might point
to the claim that our conventions 'only' regulate our talk
(thought). For according to the conventionalist, our conventions also articulate the world. The conventionalist is claiming that we cannot make any sense of modality, of essential
properties, or of identity across possible worlds independently of our conventions. The considerations of transworld
identity which are needed to make sense of the *de re / de dicto*
distinction cannot come into play without them. So it is not
as if, as is required for this realist worry to get going, there
are facts about who's who in various possible worlds and our
conventions then merely determine which of these things are
to be called by the same name or fall under the same predicate, but rather that these decisions (or at least some of them)
determine who's who. If a name is used rigidly, the things to
which it applies are *thereby* identical. We may explain how we
can generate truths *de re,* then, by saying either that our
conventions do not merely regulate how we talk, or by saying that the metaphysical facts on which the possibility of *de
re* truths depends are not separable from how we talk. However we describe it, the conventionalist is able to produce *de
re* modal truths because, on his view, our conventions cut a
lot deeper than our opponent (above) gives them credit for,
and they can do so because it is not merely the modal facts
that result from our conventions, but the individuals and
kinds that are modally involved.

Modal truths *de re,* then, as the necessary *a posteriori,* do not
settle the issue between realists and conventionalists. The
conventionalist has an account, and the realist can thus not

simply point to these modal phenomena. By the same token, the conventionalist need not deny that there are such phenomena. While he may have good independent reason for rejecting arguments for the claim that some necessary truth is *de re*, or that some *a posteriori* truth is necessary, he should not feel that there must be something wrong with these arguments if conventionalism is true. By showing that the conventionalist can offer such an account, I hope to move the debate to its proper arena. The issue between realists and conventionalists is not over what sorts of necessary truths there are, be they *a posteriori* or *de re*. It is over the grounds of necessity and the explanation of modal phenomena. In the next chapter, I will finally turn directly to this topic and argue that, on both metaphysical and epistemological grounds, the conventionalist account is superior to the realist's. Having argued that we can be empiricists about modality, even with necessity *a posteriori* and *de re*, I will now argue that we should be empiricists.

Final Remark: Intentions, Conventions,
and Their Representation

As anyone with the goodwill and patience to have read through this chapter is undoubtedly aware, the sorts of conventions to which I have suggested the conventionalist should appeal are hardly the sort of thing one would expect to hear spilling out of the mouth of an ordinary, competent speaker of English. Normal speakers are not really up on the use/mention and formal/material differences that are crucial to the adequacy of the account, and it hardly seems plausible that most competent speakers have the concept of rigid designation. It thus may seem that, even if we have provided a possible conventionalist account, this is so only in the broadest sense of 'possible'. Quite independently of its metaphysical merits or detractions, it is completely implausible that my proposed conventions could govern the use of this portion of English.

While this concern raises some very interesting general issues about philosophical method, I will confine myself to a short, two-part response. First, I doubt that there is any impropriety in attributing to ordinary speakers the concept of rigid designation, or at least the ability to intend to use a term rigidly. No doubt they are mostly unfamiliar with the *term*, and it might take quite a while to get them to understand it. But if someone says 'The president of the United States is essentially human', and does not consider the possibility of a woman president (while admitting that it is indeed possible) to count against his claim, then it would seem that he was using 'The president of the United States' rigidly, and presumably in virtue of intending to do so. If one can use modal language, then all that is needed to intend to use a term rigidly is an ability to judge, or to say, whether certain states of affairs would count for or against one's modal claims, and for these judgments, in turn, to be informed by judgments about whether the entities in these possible states of affairs are the same or not. And even this need not be especially articulate. We may be able to see, even if the speaker does not, whether his judgments about the relevance of some possible states of affairs to some modal claim are guided by his views about the identity of the parts of those states of affairs. And insofar as they are, there seems nothing inappropriate with saying that such a speaker is using some term rigidly in that claim.

While we are able to spell out pretty easily in this case what sorts of abilities a speaker needs in order to intend to use a term rigidly, I think we do well to be in general suspicious of claims skeptical about what sort of concepts ordinary speakers are able to employ. Being sensitive to a distinction does not require being articulate about it. When we philosophers use our own technical vocabulary to ascribe intentions or describe conventions, we are hardly saying that these are the descriptions an ordinary speaker would recognize as such. All we are claiming is that the distinctions that we are marking are ones to which ordinary speakers are somehow sensitive. If we are right, this seems sufficient to ascribe these concepts to the speakers, or at least for the claim that speakers have these intentions (or that we as a community have a certain convention) not to be ruled out of court as wildly false. In our case, what seems hardly plausible is that ordinary speakers are *not* able to make these distinctions. If they weren't, the very plausibility that there are necessary truths *a posteriori* or *de re* would be undermined.

This aside, we may turn to the second part of our reply. This is to acknowledge that we are engaged in a certain amount of rational reconstruction, as presumably is anyone who wishes to explain what seems ontologically noxious to him in terms of our conventions. Our need to ascend to the formal mode in the formulation of our conventions earlier in this chapter was informed directly by the inability of material mode formulations to produce necessary *a posteriori* truths that could be understood as modally grounded in our conventions. It does seem hardly likely that even an especially articulate ordinary speaker would take such care in formulating his intentions. But the ordinary speaker—we in our ordinary speech—is not trying to explain what is necessary or possible, but to say what is so. Now, an ordinary speaker, *even if he thinks he is introducing a modal distinction where there is none*, is most unlikely to say or think anything beyond, say, 'Let's call something 'water', in any possible situation, just in case it has the same deep structure as this'. Suppose, now, that we come to consider it to be necessary *a posteriori* that water is H_2O, but that we do not think that there is any real necessity. It then turns out that we have to go through the somewhat complex song and dance which I've been tapping in this chapter. In a way, I haven't been appealing to anything more than the sort of intention just described. But described this way, it is not adequate to make it true that water is necessarily H$_2$O, without the presupposition of real necessity. And worse, as we've seen, if there is no real necessity, this sort of intention on behalf of the linguistic community would serve only to leave them with a bunch of empty terms. In short, while it does not seem inappropriate to ascribe these intentions to ordinary speakers, their having them will not allow them to do what they want to do and think they are doing with these terms. Insofar as we do not think that these terms are empty, and we do think that we've got necessary *a posteriori* truths, the conventionalist plugs the gap in the way discussed in this chapter. Saying that we have these conventions is not designed for psychological reality. It is an attempt to reconstruct the intentions speakers have in such a way that they may achieve what they want to achieve and what they think they have achieved. Put slightly differently, we may say that, insofar as we have a desire to carve the world up, with modal import, according to its deep features (for instance), and it turns out to be true that water is necessarily H$_2$O, then the conventions we have described represent how the terms must be governed if there is in fact no real necessity. While no one is being said to formulate any complex intentions in the formal mode, still, we regulate our counterfactual ascriptions of 'water' by sameness of microstructure with most (enough) of the items we actually call (by which we introduced) 'water', and the fact that we behave in this way—at least, in the absence of real necessity—is sufficient for us to say that we have a convention that is properly formulated in the formal manner we discussed earlier.

In brief, it is not the job of the ordinary speaker to theorize about what he is doing, or to have a deep view about how it is being accomplished. Our common thoughts about these matters may be full of misconceptions, and they may well enter into the way in which we formulate what we are trying to do in our use of certain words. This does not prevent us from succeeding in what we try to do, or at least, as philosophers, we should be charitable in attributing mechanisms that allow us to succeed, at least where there is no special reason for denying that we have. The conventions that we ascribe to a linguistic community need not merely reflect the group's coordinated intentions, but may reflect a larger portion of their linguistic behavior, charitably formulated.

In sum, then, I hope to have shown in this chapter that, despite apparent difficulties and the threat of presupposing real necessity, the account outlined in chap. 2 actually does represent the possibility of a conventionalist explanation of the necessary *a posteriori*. In the next chapter, I will argue that the conventionalist account is not only possible but true.

4 The Case for Conventionalism and the Problem with Real Necessity

TO THIS POINT, I have argued that the recent findings of the necessary *a posteriori* and *de re* necessities entail neither that there is real necessity or real essences, nor, consequently, that the fundamental empiricist position concerning necessity and essence (or, then, kinds and individuals) is false. For all the recent hubbub, all necessity could still be rooted in convention, and kinds (and maybe individuals) could still be, in an important way, creatures of the understanding.

But it may be justly objected that while these findings do not entail a realist understanding of these matters, they do lend it great support and greatly shake the grounds for the conventionalist view. All I have done is present a model, a way out for the empiricist, a straw at which to grasp. What reason have we to present the picture I have presented? Indeed, do we not have good reason to reject it? After all, my model appeals to analyticity and, worse, analyticity of a systematically important kind. Is this not reason for great suspicion?

This chapter and the next respond to these worries. I argue that we have reason to accept my account simply insofar as it preserves the conventional nature of necessity. Real necessity is something we would need to be forced into accepting, and, as we have seen, the support for it is not strong enough for this. This line gives rise to the retort, "But isn't analyticity just as problematic?" The first thing to say here is that if analyticity is unacceptable, then so are necessary truths *a posteriori*, for I shall argue that consideration of these synthetic modalities leads directly to the finding of analytic principles of a more general nature. In the next chapter, however, I shall offer two further sorts of response. First, I shall argue that the reasons typically adduced in attacks upon analyticity are not of a sort that can justify a strategy of simply rejecting any claims that commit us to analyticity, nor do they justify a completely thoroughgoing skepticism. Second, I shall argue that there *must* be analyticity somewhere among individuative principles. This argument should lend independent support to my claim that there are analytic (general) principles of individuation central to our conceptual scheme, and that it is they that are the source of the recently found necessities. Finally, it is worth emphasizing that if my argument from necessity is correct, then even if my defenses of analyticity do not work, the proper conclusion is not that there is real necessity or that I am wrong to claim that necessities *a posteriori* require grounding in analytic truths, but rather that there are no necessary truths *a posteriori*. For (1) given the problem with real necessity, any reason to believe that something is a necessary truth is reason to believe that its necessity is grounded in analyticity, and (2) as we shall see, consideration of necessities *a posteriori* leads independently quite directly to analytic principles of individuation.

The Argument from Necessity

We were led to our discussion of general principles of individuation and to the suggestion that they are analytic by asking whether necessary truths *a posteriori* are conclusive evidence of there being real necessity. This inquiry was motivated by the long-standing view that all necessity is grounded in our conventions, a view in turn motivated by a worry as to how there could be real necessity or even whether the notion makes sense. If these concerns are well founded, then we have good reason to accept the picture I have presented; this I call 'the argument from necessity'. Given necessary truths *a posteriori*, if there are not analytic general principles of individuation,[1] then there is real necessity. Since there is no real necessity, there are analytic general principles of individuation.

But some may wonder about this argument. Why the skepticism about real necessity? Some people will be inclined to think either that there is no more reason to think that general principles of individuation are analytic than that they are synthetic, or else that there is good reason to think they are synthetic, insofar as analyticity is generally problematic.

Now, I find it hard to believe that there are people who do not find the notion of real necessity either incomprehensible or at least extremely troublesome. I believe that anyone thinking about it for a short while will be quite unsympathetic to the notion of real necessity, unless presented with philosophical arguments to the contrary. Interestingly, our most distinguished opponent of essentialism, W. V. O. Quine, nowhere bothers to argue against the view. In attacking modal logic, he argues that

> The way to do quantified modal logic, if at all, is to accept Aristotelian essentialism. To defend Aristotelian essentialism, however, is not part of my plan. Such a philosophy is as unreasonable by my lights as it is by Carnap's or Lewis's.[2]

---

[1] Or, more generally, analytic individuative principles, since, as indicated in chap. 3, these need not be general.

[2] W. V. O. Quine, "Reference and Modality," in *From a Logical Point of View* (Cambridge: Harvard University Press, 1953), p. 156.

and

> There is yet a further consequence (of quantified modal logic)
> and a particularly sticky one: Aristotelian essentialism . . .
> [q]uantified modality . . . leads us back into the jungle of Ar-
> istotelian essentialism.[3]

Quine takes it as sufficient to argue that quantified modal
logic commits us to essentialism; it is unnecessary to complete the argument with an attack on that doctrine. Its mere
mention, we may suppose, is expected to send shivers down
the spines of our ontological sensibilities. And of course, he is
not alone in this opinion.

Yet I know that there are people who do not share this
intuition with Quine, the empiricists, and myself. For this
reason, I shall try to give some account of the intuition that
there is no real necessity and, thus, to support the argument
from necessity on behalf of my conventionalist explanation
of the necessary *a posteriori*.

The Problem with Real Necessity:
The Epistemological Problem

1. We believe not only that there are necessary truths, but
that we know what some of them are. And we believe not
merely that we know the truths, but that we know them to
be necessary. We know that the truths of mathematics are
necessary, we know that it is necessary that bachelors are
unmarried, and it has recently been made plausible that we
know it to be necessary that water is H_2O.

This knowledge of ours is somewhat problematic. How
can we know that something is not only true, but that it is

---

[3]W. V. O. Quine, "Three Grades of Modal Involvement," in *The Ways
of Paradox* (Cambridge: Harvard University Press, 1966), pp. 175–76.

necessarily so? What is our access to other possible worlds in virtue of which we know that in none of them is some actual truth false? But these questions should not drive us to despair, for we do know that some things are true necessarily. What we should do is turn our attention to the matter of how we actually come by this knowledge. Only if our methods seem inadequate to the task should we become skeptical.

It is to this epistemological issue that we now turn. I shall argue that our methods can be understood to give us modal knowledge only if the 'modal structure of the world' is closely tied to our conventions; our methods cannot give us knowledge of a completely independent reality, but only of the limits of our conceptual scheme. Thus, I claim, we must reckon the necessary truths of which we actually have knowledge as dependent upon our conventions for their necessity.

2. Traditionally, reasoning about what is possible or necessary has been undertaken by considering what we can imagine, or thought experiments more generally. It is a commonplace in philosophical argument to reject a proposed criterion for something by claiming that one can imagine the condition failing to hold in the presence of that for which it is supposed to be criterial. Indeed, the supposition that what is imaginable is possible is so fundamental to philosophical discussion that the move from 'x is imaginable' to 'x is possible' is usually not made explicit—we go straight from the imaginability of a proposition's negation to the denial of its necessity.

Similarly, claims to necessity are supported by judgments that we cannot imagine what it would be like for the proposition in question to be false. This is a bit more difficult, for it can be claimed against this that we have not tried hard enough. Here we face a difficulty common to the evaluation of all nonexistence claims. However, what we do in order to support claims that a proposition is necessary is try to imagine situations in which it seems most likely that the proposition would be false if it is ever false. So, when testing whether it is necessary that bachelors are unmarried, we may consider a married man who lives apart from his wife, has little or no contact with her, goes on many dates, eats macaroni and cheese, and so on, living a typical bachelor life. We try to give him all the typical properties of a bachelor and consider whether, for all that, his being married still prevents him from being a bachelor—which it does. We may sometimes fortify our claims by pointing to a 'mental cramp' (to use Wittgenstein's phrase) that arises when we try to imagine the proposition's being false. In addition, we may try to derive a proposition from others already known to be necessary (or possible), for instance, from the truths of logic. However, our justification for believing that these conclusions are necessary (possible) will still derive, in part, from our support for believing the premises to be necessary, and, at bottom (I hope this is uncontroversial), we shall always find appeals to imagination or thought experiments.

As long as we think of this as the methodology of modal inquiry, we have good reason to accept a conventionalist view about necessity. For if one thinks that there are real necessities, that, for instance, things have essences quite independently of how we think or talk about them, then the role of imagination in modal inquiry will seem quite mysterious. Not only will it seem implausible that imaginability entails possibility, but it will be unclear why we should think that there is even a relation of good evidence. The realist must either find some connection between our imaginations and the modal structure of the world, or else find some further basis upon which we can legitimately ground our judgments about possibility and necessity—and this we do not seem to find in actual cases. Suppose, though, that all necessary truths are analytic. We ought then to be able to derive a contradiction, or at least a linguistically inadmissible assertion,[4] from

---

[4]Not all linguistically inadmissible assertions—analytic falsehoods—are contradictions (in the syntactic sense), for instance, 'This box is both red all

the negation of a necessary truth. If we cannot derive a contradiction from an assertion, we may assume that it is not analytically false, hence not necessarily false, and thus possible. But it is just the linguistic rules that determine necessity and possibility that also constrain how we may describe the contents of our imaginations. To say that we cannot imagine that p is false is to say that we cannot think of circumstances in which we would deny that p. Similarly, when we say that we can imagine that p, we assert that there is nothing incoherent in the thought that p. Thus, if one thinks that necessity amounts to analyticity, it is fairly straightforward how possibility should follow from imaginability. We do not grant that contradictions can properly describe imaginations, but that is the only constraint upon what we can imagine. Contradictoriness is the boundary both of what is possible and also of what is imaginable.

It is worth noting also, in passing, that the view that necessity is analyticity does not require that imagination be essential to our modal inquiries. It is just that, insofar as imagination does play this role, we have reason to think that the sort of reality about which we are learning has more to do with how we think than with how the world independently is. This conclusion would be warranted even if, as may sometimes be the case, we cannot point to particular imaginative exercises involved, so long as our method of inquiry does not seem to be a way of finding out about the world apart from us.

But all this seems to be thrown into confusion by the

---

over and green all over (and not one painted on top of the other)'. It is this failure of all necessary (analytic) falsehoods to be reducible to syntactic contradictions that in large measure moved Wittgenstein away from the *Tractatus* and toward the *Investigations* (see his "Some Remarks on Logical Form," *Proceedings of the Aristotelian Society Supplement*, vol. 9 [1929]: pp. 162–71). At any rate, if by 'contradiction' one is willing to include falsehoods *not* reducible to syntactic contradictions, the qualification in the text is unnecessary. For this reason, I shall hence use 'contradiction' in this looser sense.

establishing of the necessary *a posteriori*. For one thing, it overturns the equation of necessity with analyticity. 'Water is H_2O' is not analytic, nor is 'Hesperus is Phosphorus'. Thus, the account of modality that was to explain the role of imagination in our modal inquiries is false and so cannot explain anything. Further, the role of imagination itself is cast into doubt. For it seems that we can imagine that there is water that is not H_2O—indeed, we can imagine that our water is not H_2O, or at least we can conceive of finding out that it is not.[5] Imaginability does not entail possibility.

This separation of imaginability from possibility is not surprising once we note that necessity is not analyticity. If what is possible is not determined by the confines of our concepts, then there is no reason to think that our imaginations, the limits of which *are* determined by our concepts, will show us what is possible. And this may be thought to support realists about necessity, since they do not think that imaginability entails possibility and, further, do not even see how there could (or should) be a significant connection. Though this point about imagination by no means entails their position, it is something that they can claim we should expect. In addition, it supports their position in a negative way by removing a troubling objection. For if imaginability does not entail

---

[5]Or, if we cannot imagine this, then we do not always imagine what we seem to imagine. One of the following principles must go: (1) We always imagine what we seem to imagine or (2) Imaginability entails possibility. I am not sure that there is a real issue over which to reject. What is important is that what we seem to imagine is not always possible, and that the difference between seeming to imagine and imagining—if there is one—is not available to introspection. Thus, even if imaginability *does* still entail possibility, imagination cannot be relied upon as a method, for we cannot tell when we are imagining something and when we only seem to do so. I shall henceforward describe the troublesome phenomenon as 'imagining the impossible', thus rejecting (2); this should be understood as an arbitrary choice adopted for convenience. Whatever I say about imaginings can be translated, if one prefers to reject (1), into claims about seeming imaginings without loss in the substance of my discussion.

possibility, it cannot be objected that they cannot explain why it does entail possibility. There is no need to explain what is not the case.

But things are not so simple. For we are still—or newly— owed an account of the epistemology of necessity. We certainly cannot advocate realism on the grounds of necessary truths *a posteriori* if there is no explanation of how we come to know that such truths are necessary. More generally, we need to know what replaces or supplements imagination as a guide to modal reality. The necessary *a posteriori* may throw our earlier conclusions into doubt, but it does not provide us with a solution to our inquiry or a reason to abandon it. It merely raises new puzzles.

3. As before, the most natural way to approach the problem is to consider how we in fact come to know of necessary truths which are *a posteriori* that they are necessary.

Consider 'Hesperus is Phosphorus'. The easy part comes from ignoring the modal aspects temporarily. Stargazers may be able to predict the positions of planetary bodies at various times in the day. The chart for a certain body seen in the morning matches that for one seen in the evening: Presto. They are the same body.

The actual stories may be interesting, but they are not really relevant to the problem at hand. What matters is that however the discovery is made, the modal conclusion—that the proposition is necessary—will not be warranted by this evidence. The empirical evidence for the proposition is insufficient to establish that it is necessarily true (I do not at this point mean to claim that what in addition is needed may not itself be empirical.). Something else is needed. And indeed, in all cases of knowledge of necessities *a posteriori*, something else is present. Let us look at some actual arguments.

Waiving fussy considerations deriving from the fact that x need not have necessary existence, it was clear from $(x) \ \Box \ (x = x)$ and Leibniz's law that identity is an 'internal' relation:

$(x)(y)(x = y \supset \Box \, x = y)$. (What pairs (x,y) could be counter-examples? Not pairs of distinct objects, for then the antecedent is false; nor any pair of an object and itself, for then the consequent is true.) If 'a' and 'b' are rigid designators, it follows that '$a = b$', if true, is a necessary truth. If 'a' and 'b' are *not* rigid designators, no such conclusion follows about the *statement* '$a = b$' (though the *objects* designated by 'a' and 'b' will be necessarily identical).[6]

Can we imagine a situation in which it would have happened that this very woman [Queen Elizabeth] came out of Mr. and Mrs. Truman? . . . How could a person originating from different parents, from a totally different sperm and egg, be *this very woman*? One can imagine, *given* the woman, that various things in her life could have changed. . . . But what is harder to imagine is her being born of different parents. It seems to me that anything coming from a different origin would not be this object.[7]

A principle suggested by these examples is: *If a material object has its origin from a certain hunk of matter, it could not have had its origin in any other matter.* . . . [I]n a large class of cases the principle is perhaps susceptible of something like a proof, using the principle of the necessity of identity for particulars.[8]

Kripke offers us considerations in defense of the necessity of identity and the essentiality of origin. In neither case does he appeal to scientific or even ordinary observations or empirical discoveries. In the first instance, Kripke appeals to the fact that an object is necessarily identical to itself, and derives a general principle (Kripke was not, of course, the first to offer such a derivation). If the general principle is true at all, it is certainly knowable *a priori*. No empirical considerations

[6]Kripke, *Naming and Necessity*, p. 3.
[7]Ibid., pp. 112–13.
[8]Ibid., p. 114; n. 56; see also n. 57.

have entered. It is the general principle that explains the necessity of particular identities, such as, Hesperus = Phosphorus, and forms the basis upon which we know of their necessity. This bit of *a priori* knowledge is what allows us to conclude, given our empirical evidence, that Hesperus is not only identical to Phosphorus, but that it is necessarily so. But we have already claimed that the empirical evidence is, of itself, insufficient for the modal conclusion. So this *a priori* principle is crucial. But such principles tell us nothing of the independent world.[9] The conclusion, then, should be that the factual, or empirical, content of 'Hesperus is necessarily identical to Phosphorus' and kindred truths is nothing beyond that of 'Hesperus is identical to Phosphorus'. Our empirical considerations can yield no more, and our knowledge of the principle that can yield more is nonfactual. Our methods for ascertaining knowledge of necessity are not methods for learning about the world.

Similar remarks apply to Kripke's defense of the essentiality of origin. In his 'proof' (note 56) he appeals to nothing at all empirical. The only factual consideration is the hypothesis that a table *B* in fact originates in piece of wood *A*. The argument to the conclusion that this origin is necessary relies on purely philosophical considerations. It is extremely difficult to see how this method for coming to know of necessity could be a procedure for learning anything about the world. As before, it is only our procedures for ascertaining the nonmodalized truths that seem capable of revealing the way the

[9]One should believe this even if one thinks there can be contingent *a priori* knowledge. Instances of such knowledge, if such there be, will be quite limited in contrast with general principles and will not, at any rate, give us knowledge that is quite independent of our thoughts or conventions. See Philip Kitcher, "*A Priori* Knowledge," *Philosophical Review* 89 (1981): 3–23, and Keith Donnellan, "The Contingent *A Priori* and Rigid Designators," in P. French, T. Uehling and H. Wettstein eds., *Contemporary Perspectives in the Philosophy of Language* (Minneapolis: University of Minnesota Press, 1979).

world is. Our methods could not tell us about the modal status of these truths if necessity were an independent feature of the world.

It is worth noting that these considerations support not only the claim that our knowledge is not of real necessity, but the claim that general principles of individuation are analytic. Of course, they do so derivatively, in accordance with our earlier argument that, if there is no real necessity, then general principles of individuation must be analytic. But the claim about general principles is here also supported directly, since the essentiality of origin is such a general principle, and the arguments on its behalf are *a priori* and based on considerations of what we can imagine.

But surely we can do better. There must be other, more empirical methods we employ in coming to know of necessary truths. Why don't we look at the hard cases? Don't Kripke and Putnam say that it is science that reveals to us the natures of things, that is, their essences?

> Let us suppose that scientists have investigated the nature of gold and have found that it is part of the very nature of this substance, so to speak, that it have atomic number 79.[10]

> The key point is that the relation same$_L$ (a cross-world relation determining kind membership) is a *theoretical* relation: whether something is or is not the same liquid as *this* may take an indeterminate amount of scientific investigation to determine.[11]

Since these scientific findings are supposed to either be or at least entail statements like 'Gold essentially has atomic number 79' and 'Water is necessarily H_2O', we ought to look at how these conclusions are reached. This would appear

[10]Kripke, *Naming and Necessity*, p. 124.
[11]Putnam, "The Meaning of 'Meaning'," p. 225.

to be our best bet for finding the empirical discovery of necessity.

But even a brief look here should make it clear that the situation is just the same as it is in the cases we have considered. Scientists can discover, by whatever methods they have, that samples of water are composed of H_2O and even that all water is so composed; similarly, they can come to know the atomic structure of gold. But is there anything in their procedure that could reveal to them that water is *necessarily* H_2O or that gold *necessarily* has atomic number 79? They could determine, no doubt, that these microstructural features were the causally most important of the kinds that they underlie, but this falls short of the the modal knowledge for which we are looking. As before, however, I think we have little difficulty in isolating what it is that could, and does, allow us to come to know that these underlying features are essential to their kinds.

Take the case of water's being H_2O. I agree that we do not judge this to be necessary on the grounds that we cannot imagine its negation—for we can imagine (seem to imagine) water without H_2O.[12] However, this is not to say that imagination does not come into the picture. Insofar as the necessity is argued for at all, it is argued for on the grounds that we cannot imagine both that water is actually H_2O *and* that something that is not H_2O, in some counterfactual situation, is water (or, if the wording is offensive, that we cannot imagine something that is not H_2O being water given the supposition that water actually is H_2O). It is not that imagination does not play the crucial role in our judgments about what is necessary; it is just that the sorts of imagining that are in-

[12]See n. 5. If we *cannot* imagine water without H_2O (because whatever is imaginable is possible), our *knowledge* that we cannot is *subsequent* to our knowledge that water is necessarily H_2O. It should be clear that this sort of unimaginability, which is compatible with seeming imaginability, cannot form the grounds for our judgments that something is necessary.

volved are somewhat more complex than we have typically thought—they are imaginings *given* empirical suppositions.

> Once we have discovered that water is H_2O, nothing counts as a possible world in which water isn't H_2O.[13]

> Suppose that all the areas which actually contain gold now, contained pyrites instead, or some other substance which counterfeited the superficial properties of gold but lacked its atomic structure. Would we say, of this counterfactual situation, that in that situation gold would not have been an element (because pyrites is not an element)? It seems to me that we would not.[14]

Simple reflection, as well as a glimpse at the literature, should show that this will always be the case in arguments that some empirical fact is necessary. Empirical investigations may show us that the fact obtains, but our judgment that it is necessary depends on our not being able to imagine the state of affairs not obtaining given that it actually does; the justification for believing that the state of affairs obtains is empirical, but our justification for believing that it is necessary is not. Notice that these thought experiments do not depend upon anything empirical—we do not have to believe anything one way or the other about the state of affairs we 'suppose' to obtain. We merely ask: What do we say about these counterfactual cases *if* this fact obtains? And it will also be noted that what we find in these reflections is not a particular fact that will be necessary if true, but a whole class.[15] Whatever we suppose to be the chemical composition of water will be such that we cannot, on this supposition, imagine something to be water that lacks this composition.

---

[13]Putnam, "The Meaning of 'Meaning'," p. 233.

[14]Kripke, *Naming and Necessity*, p. 124.

[15]Again, we need not suppose that this *needs* to be the case, only that it is plausible that it is.

Similarly, we will uphold the possibility of what we imagine if this is done on the supposition that what is imagined is in fact false. Thus, while we will not grant that it is possible for water not to be H_2O just because we can (seem to) imagine this, we will concede its possibility if we can still imagine this on the supposition that water *is* H_2O. Arguments against empirical necessities must take this more complex form: Imagining the proposition false while granting its actual truth.[16] These imaginings, I maintain, entail the possibility of what is imagined. Our situation is just as traditionally viewed, but with a wrinkle about empirical suppositions.

Given that thought experiments and the imagination are still crucial to our modal investigations, the grounds I earlier claimed they provided for the rejection of realism about necessity are still with us. Unless the realist can tell us what access imagination can give us to a separate and independently existing modal reality, we must conclude that modality is somehow a product of our conventions. Perhaps the implausibility of expecting such an account can be seen from noticing that we do not think the testimony of the imagination gives us any clue at all as to what is *physically* necessary or possible. This is no surprise—such modalities are determined by laws of nature, and these can be revealed only through empirical research. But why, then, should we think that we can learn about metaphysical modalities through the imagination? We should expect imagination to be a good guide, I think, only if these broader modalities are determined not metaphysically, but cognitively—in particular, by our conventions.

But this gives rise to a possible realist rejoinder. The inability of realists to give an account of how our appeals to imagination justify our claims about what is necessary gives us reason to accept a conventionalist account only if conventionalism does not also founder in attempting to provide an

[16]Of course, showing the proposition to be *actually* false will suffice.

explanation for our knowledge. And it is not obvious that it will not, once we have understood that necessity is not analyticity. Though imaginability plays a central role in our modal reasoning, the way in which it supports our claims is more complex than has traditionally been supposed. What is imaginable is not thereby possible, and when we notice the further intricacies that go into our modal judgments, it is not clear that we can get a conventionalist account that will explain not merely how imagination can be relevant to our coming to know about modality, but why it does so in such an odd manner. The neatness of our earlier account is no longer available, and we cannot just assume that there is a simple modification to be made. We need to see an account before we can say, given the role of imagination in supporting our modal claims, that conventionalism about necessity is thereby more plausible than realism.

4. But there is such an account. As we noted, it is not surprising that the views that necessity is analyticity and that imaginability entails possibility fall together. If necessity is not analyticity, then the constraints upon what we can imagine are not the same as those upon what is possible; there are impossibilities other than contradictions. However, noting this connection may allow us to use our modified conventionalist explanation of necessity to explain the role of imagination in our coming to have modal knowledge, and how it is that this gives us knowledge.

The conventionalist's response to the necessary *a posteriori* and the concomitant rejection of the view that necessity is analyticity, I argued earlier, should be to appeal to general principles of individuation. If it is analytic that chemical compounds have their chemical compositions necessarily, then while it is synthetic that water is H_2O (as well as that this is necessary), the necessity of this is explained by our convention. While necessity is not equated with analyticity, it is still explained by it—or, at least, by the content of (some of) our analytic truths; necessity may still, perhaps, be equated with something like analyticity, that is, inability to be denied without violating our linguistic conventions. Of course, we do not straightforwardly violate a convention by denying that water is H_2O, for this is not an analytic truth. However, we do violate a convention by denying that it is necessary that water is H_2O while affirming that water is H_2O.[17] We might, then, say that synthetic necessity is a property of a proposition such that one violates a linguistic rule if one both affirms the truth of the proposition and affirms the possibility of its falsehood (that is, denies that the proposition holds in some other world when presented with some counterfactual situation)—and the proposition is true.[18]

It is not at present worth pursuing whether or not this is, or could be made into, an adequate 'definition' of synthetic necessity. What is important to notice is that we can understand how synthetic necessary truths may arise from our conventions, and to see that the nature of these conventions is such that they do not, of themselves, specify what is necessary, but only what is necessary given certain conditions (that is, given what is actually the case). It is this feature, of course, that allows the necessary truths themselves to be synthetic.

But now we see something very interesting. Given the peculiarities in the way in which considerations of imaginability support modal claims, we should, if we are nonrealists about necessity, expect something with just the structure

[17]This is an approximation. What is a violation depends upon what the convention is like. Thus, in addition to affirming that water is H_2O, we may have to add that this is the chemical composition of water, or that this is the fundamental underlying structure of water, or perhaps that this is its deepest explanatory feature in order to generate a contradiction. See below.

[18]This last clause is needed since one violates the same rule in denying the necessity of water's being H_2O by denying that water is necessarily H_3O, on the supposition that it is actually H_3O. The rule itself does not establish the necessary truth, but only the conditional (if p, then necessarily p). Obviously, then, it is a further condition on being a synthetic necessity that a proposition be *true*.

of these general principles to explain empirical necessities. When we defend the necessity of a synthetic truth, we see what we can imagine *upon the supposition* of that truth, and when we affirm that something we have imagined is possible, this is because we can still imagine that thing on the supposition that what we have imagined is in fact false (or, conversely, when we deny the possibility of something that we have imagined, it is because we would not be able to imagine that thing if we knew it was in fact false). More abstractly, we can defend particular necessary truths only when we can defend a more general set of conditionals: If p, then necessarily p;[19] and these conditionals are such that we cannot imagine their falsity—or more precisely, they are such that we cannot imagine the falsity of p (in some other world) given the supposition that p (in the actual world). Thus, what is established by the imagination is not that it is necessary that water is H_2O, but that if water is H_2O, this is necessary; similarly, these imaginative exercises establish that if water is H_3O, this is necessary, or if it is H_4O, and so on. What is established by the imagination is a string of conditionals, or perhaps a general principle from which they all follow. But these are just our general principles of individuation, or consequences of them! What our imagination gives us information about are our linguistic conventions. Our imaginations are guides to what is possible or necessary only upon empirical suppositions, because our conventions are such as to *make* what is possible or necessary so only given empirical facts. Thus, what we need to know, in order to know what is empirically necessary, is some empirical fact plus our conventions that tell us which truths are necessary given which empirical facts, or, alternatively, which types of

[19]Given the discussion of chap. 3, the relevant conditionals might be more perspicuously schematized: If p, then necessarily q; rather than 'If water is H_2O, it is necessarily H_2O', we have 'If (most of) the stuff we call 'water' is composed of H_2O, then necessarily, water is H_2O' (or '"water' rigidly designates H_2O', i.e., necessarily, 'water' refers to H_2O; or something from which we can derive 'necessarily, water is H_2O').

statements are necessary given which type of empirical fact. If we assume that we have analytic general principles of individuation, and that they explain the modal component of empirical necessities, then we can see why what we can or cannot imagine provides us with modal knowledge (because our imaginations tell us what our conventions are), as well as why they do so in the way in which they do (because our conventions do not of themselves determine what is necessary).

Our conventions take a conditional form: they tell us what to say *if* some empirical condition is satisfied. But if we do not know whether the condition is satisfied, we do not know what the rule tells us to say, or, more coarsely, the rule does not give us any instructions. The rules do not say 'Only if something is H_2O is it water', but 'If water is H_2O, then something is water only if it is H_2O'. If we do not know, then, whether water is H_2O, we do not make a linguistic mistake in calling something 'water' that is not H_2O. Thus, we can imagine that there is water that is not H_2O so long as we are ignorant of the facts, even though it is necessary that water is H_2O. This is why we can imagine the impossible.[20] But armed with the supposition that water is in fact H_2O, we cannot imagine that it may fail to be so. The same holds for the supposition that water is H_3O—this is why the imagination must be supplemented by empirical data in order to reach conclusions about what is necessary. But this factual supplement is just what must also be added to our conventions in order to determine what is necessary. What we need to know, beyond what is established by the imagination, in order to know what is necessary, is just what must be true, beyond our conventions, in order to make it (synthetically)[21] necessary.

[20]Or, if one has opted to hold onto imaginability entailing possibility, read 'This is why we can *seem* to imagine the impossible'.

[21]If something is analytically necessary, nothing empirical needs to be added to our conventions to make it necessary.

When we assume that we have analytic general principles of individuation, we find that we are able to give as complete and fully explanatory an account of the role of imagination in modal inquiry as we were able to give when it was supposed that all necessary truths are analytic. The basic story in the explanation is the same: what we can imagine is determined by our conventions, and these same conventions determine what is necessary and possible. The difference between the stories arises from the difference between the type of conventions invoked—general principles of individuation take a hypothetical form. Our imaginations can thus inform us only of these conditionals; our 'nonconditional' imaginings, or imaginings not on empirical suppositions, can establish possibility only if they can be maintained on the supposition that what is imagined is actually false, for only then are they 'crucial tests' as regards the conventions that determine modalities.[22] Similarly, the conventions themselves determine what is modally the case in conditional form; as with the imagination, the determination of modality requires an empirical component. Again, it is precisely where empirical facts come into determining what is modally the case that imagination may fail as a guide to modality. Insofar as we keep to consideration of conditionals, what we can or cannot imagine functions exactly as we thought it did when we thought all necessity was analytic. When we see what our conventions are like, we can explain both why appeals to imagination are epistemically relevant and why such appeals need to be complicated. Consideration of our solution to the conventionalist's problem with necessities *a posteriori* allows us to solve his problem with our knowledge of such truths and also allows us to see that these necessities do not create the epistemological headache for the conventionalist they may be thought to. The

---

[22]Of course, if we cannot even *suppose* that something is false, then it is itself analytic and not merely the antecedent of an analytic conditional; this truth will be necessary *a priori*.

epistemological data are just what we would expect to find if we believed that necessities *a posteriori* are to be explained by reference to analytic general principles of individuation; correspondingly, the epistemological account is but a minor reworking of that of the traditional empiricist.

It is also worth noting that there may be some quibbling over whether we really can imagine what is impossible (see note 5). It is sometimes claimed, for instance, that when we seem to imagine water that is not H_2O, we really imagine something very similar to, but not really, water, and that this stuff is not H_2O. Thus, we can maintain the thesis that imaginability entails possibility, but at the cost of denying that we always imagine what we seem to. What is significant is that we may have an analogous quibble over whether the fact that someone is ignorant of the truth of the antecedent of a linguistic rule excuses him from violating the rule. If we do not know the microstructure of water, do we violate the rule, 'If water is H_2O, then it is necessarily H_2O', by saying that it is possible that water not be H_2O? The quibble itself is unimportant, but notice this: It is only on the condition of ignorance that we can (seem to) imagine the impossible, and this same ignorance raises a problem about what to say concerning the violation of linguistic rules. This should hardly be surprising if the conventionalist story I have told is correct. If we think that our ignorance does not prevent us from violating a rule, we should be inclined to say that we cannot imagine the impossible—for then linguistic violation, which determines imaginability (though not seeming imaginability), would be constrained not only by our conventions, but also by the facts that combine with our conventions to determine what is possible; if, however, we think that we do not violate a rule when ignorant of the truth of its antecedent, then it is reasonable to say that we can imagine the impossible—for then, while our conventions alone determine the limits of imaginability, it is our conventions plus empirical conditions that determine the limits of possibility. What we count as imaginable, then, is tied to what we count as a linguistic violation, and while we have settled that necessity and possibility (for these cases) are definitely to be tied to the product of our conventions plus the empirical facts, we can go either way on linguistic violation and, consequently, on imaginability. Even if we were settled, it would clearly be a matter of choice, a question of whether we want the notion of imaginability to be tied to something directly epistemologically accessible, or whether we should settle for the surrogate notion of 'seeming imaginability'. This is why the issue is rather a quibble. All this, I suggest, provides additional support for the view that synthetic necessities are explained by analytic general principles of individuation; that hypothesis allows us to explain, in an interesting way, a phenomenon (the dispute over whether we can imagine the impossible, and its seemingly trivial nature) for which it was not designed as an explanation.

At any rate, I hope it is clear that our account does not really need additional support. By supposing that we have analytic principles of individuation, we can explain how it is that our methods of judging what is necessary or possible can give us knowledge, and we can do so in more than a vague way. If we suppose, however, that (all) general principles of individuation are synthetic, and that necessity is a real feature of the world, then it is extremely unclear how our methods justify us in our modal claims, and even less clear how they could give us knowledge. For what access could our investigations give us to an independent modal reality? We ought to conclude, I believe, that insofar as we have knowledge of necessity and possibility, these modal features are explained by our conventions; if we believe that there are necessary truths *a posteriori*, we ought to believe that there are analytic general principles of individuation in virtue of which their necessity can be explained. In short, we ought to be empiricists about necessity.

In Addition

We gain further support from considering another aspect
of the defense of necessary truths *a posteriori*. Consider water's being H_2O. We are supposed to be led into thinking
this to be necessary by imagining that somewhere—Twin
Earth—there is stuff that looks, tastes, and functions like
water, but that is composed of something other than H_2O.
We can imagine it as similar (observationally) to water as we
like—this stuff is rained, fills lakes, is used to make drinks
and wash clothes. We are then asked whether this stuff is
water, and we are supposed to say no. This stuff is no more
water than iron pyrites is gold, or a perfect mechanical dog is
a dog. Thus, nothing can be water that is not H_2O.

There are certainly many people who share the intuition
that Twin Earth 'water' is not really water. But this is not at
all universal. Some people say, "Sure it's water."[23] What can
be said to such a person (call him "Sly")? We might ask
whether Sly knows that actual water is composed of H_2O,
that its being H_2O accounts for its more phenomenally sa-
lient features, and that grouping substances according to their
chemical compositions generally avails us of the most fruitful
and explanatory chemical theory. He might say that he does.
Still, this Twin Earth stuff is water. A different kind of water, if you like, but water nonetheless. At this point, I maintain that we must view the argument between Sly and people
with more 'scientifically oriented' intuitions as a verbal dispute. They do not disagree about the facts; they merely use
the term 'water' differently.[24] Putnam (to give a name to a

---

[23]I trust that all readers will be familiar with some such people.

[24]They may disagree *over* the verbal facts—that is, in calling this stuff
'water', Sly is probably not simply making his own stipulation, but also
thinks that as the word 'water' is used by his linguistic community, it is
correct to call the stuff 'water'. Someone like Putnam, of course, thinks
otherwise, and this is a real dispute between them. But it is not a *metaphysi-*

scientifically oriented type) uses 'water' (and kind terms generally) to refer to whatever has the same underlying explanatory features as 'this stuff' (pointing to a glass of water), while Sly uses 'water' to refer to something else, say, whatever has a certain appearance and plays a certain role (call this 'water$_2$'). They refer to different things. The stuff Putnam refers to is not instantiated on Twin Earth; the stuff Sly refers to is. The appearance of a disagreement results not only from their using the same word, but also from the coextension of the types of stuff here (on Earth). But so long as Sly sticks to his guns, even when the deep facts about (actual) water are made clear, we cannot accuse him of metaphysical error.

Now, if the fact that water is H_2O were a real metaphysical necessity, one would think that someone who responds as Sly did would simply be wrong. He says that the Twin Earth stuff is water, but it is not. We should not understand him to be referring to some other stuff (kind, property), so that what he expresses by 'That is water' and 'Water is not necessarily H_2O' are true. We should interpret his words and ours univocally, and say that he is wrong. Or, rather, this is what we should do if we think that water's being H_2O is a metaphysical necessity. 'Water' refers to stuff of which we see actual samples, this stuff has (independent) modal properties, and one of these properties is necessarily being (composed of) H_2O. Sly is wrong to think that the Twin Earth stuff is water.

But we do not think that Sly is simply wrong. We do—or at least should—understand him to be talking about something else. This does seem to be a verbal, rather than a metaphysical, dispute—at least, when Sly is in agreement with us over all the above-mentioned facts about water. If Sly is wrong, it is only because (1) he is wrong about how other members of his linguistic community use the word 'water',

---

cal dispute over the nature of water; it is a sociolinguistic dispute over the linguistic practice of their community.

taking deep structure rather than other features as the relevant respect of similarity for cross-world ascriptions (see note 24) and (2) the semantic properties of his use of the term 'water' are determined more by the linguistic intentions of the members of his community than his own (presumably via his intention to use the term as others do). If one wishes to maintain that Sly is not only wrong, but wrong for metaphysical, as opposed to sociological reasons, one needs to show us where his mistake is. One needs to show that Sly is wrong not about how members of his community individuate water, but about how water itself is individuated (and this latter, of course, must be independent of the former). Somehow, with all the same evidence, we have got it right about the individuating features of water, while Sly is metaphysically confused. Insofar as we don't think that we can provide such an account of Sly's error, it seems that the best account of Putnam and Sly's confrontation is that it is a verbal one: either they are just using 'water' differently and do not disagree; or, if our uses of terms are sufficiently dependent upon how other speakers in our community speak, then they do express the same proposition, and one of them is wrong— but, here, their disagreement is still not metaphysical, but sociolinguistic. And insofar as we do not think that we can see Sly as making any metaphysical mistake, we do not, then, think of water's necessarily being H_2O as a metaphysical fact.

Indeed, we can see rather clearly what is going on. When we think as realists about necessity, we think of achieving determinate reference to actual individuals and kinds and of then conducting inquiries (partly imaginative) in order to learn what the modal properties of these things are. But with Sly, we do not take his report about Twin Earth as a mere expression of belief. We take it as telling us what it is that he refers to in his uses of 'water', and, in particular, that he is *not* referring to something that is necessarily H_2O. What this suggests is that our reports about what we would say (what we believe) given counterfactual circumstances have more to do with the determination of what we are referring to than with (the modal properties of) the referent itself.

Our 'modal intuitions' are not, in the first instance, beliefs about independently delineated entities, but are rather expressions of our referential intentions. That we do not think Twin Earth 'water' is water shows that we are guided in our use of 'water' by microstructure, or what we think is causally important. Sly's report shows that his uses of 'water' are not so guided. The different reports do not reflect different beliefs about water—they reflect different referential intentions. Indeed, until we know what is referred to by 'water', we cannot know whether 'water is H_2O' expresses a necessary truth. But it is only by knowing whether someone thinks that water is necessarily H_2O—or, more simply, whether he thinks that Twin Earth 'water' is water—that we can know whether with 'water' he is referring to water, water$_2$, or to something else. For in the actual world, all and only instances of water are instances of water$_2$. Thus, only by knowing (at least by implication) what someone will say in counterfactual situations can we know what it is that they are referring to. But then, it is nonsense to say that our modal intuitions are beliefs about the modal properties of familiar entities. For our modal intuitions are prior to our knowledge of what the familiar entities *are*, that is, which, of the many overlapping entities (coextensive kinds) around, it is that we refer to in our uses of a term. Our modal intuitions, then, must in the first instance reflect our referential intentions and not our beliefs about the modal properties of entities specified independently of these modal properties.

This is not simply an epistemological point. Something beyond the set of things actually called 'water' is needed to determine whether water or water$_2$ is the referent of 'water'—that is, to make it the case that one rather than the other is the referent. And this extra thing is precisely what determines what we say about Twin Earth—our referential intentions. That which makes it the case that we refer to water rather than water$_2$ is the same as that which makes it the case that we deny that the stuff on Twin Earth is water. And this thing is not the substance water, but our referential intentions. To say that Twin Earth 'water' is not water because it is not 'the same stuff as this', that is, not H$_2$O, is to get things just backwards. It is because our intentions are such as to make us deny that Twin Earth 'water' is water—because they are tied to deep structure—that our term 'water' refers to (wholes composed of) H$_2$O. The modal properties of the referents of our terms are not 'discovered' by examination of these things; they are built into the determination of reference itself.[25] Once we have achieved determinate reference, it is no longer an open question what the modal properties of a thing are—for we must settle upon them, by our choice of referential intentions, in order to achieve such reference. Our modal intuitions are tied not to the entities to which we refer, but to our intentions. This is why the 'debate' between Putnam and Sly cannot be made out as metaphysical: for them to have a metaphysical dispute, both of them would need to be able to talk about the same entity, modal properties and all, in such a way that the means whereby this reference was achieved did not itself determine the (kind of) modal features of the referent. Only then could their 'modal intuitions' be properly thought of, in the first instance, as beliefs about this entity. But this, I have just argued, cannot be done. Our counterfactual reports reflect our intentions and nothing of deeper metaphysical import.

Thus, by considering how we actually come to accept synthetic truths as necessary, and what we can say to those who fail to share our modal intuitions, we find that what these intuitions reflect is not, in the first instance, our beliefs about

[25]Though, of course, when this is done by general principles of individuation, the modal properties are specified only generally, leaving room for what may be called 'the empirical discovery of essence'.

the modal properties of independently specified entities, but rather the referential intentions in virtue of which we refer to things with one rather than another set of modal properties. When we consult our modal intuitions, what we are doing is not metaphysics, but psychology or semantics. Once again, the necessity of which we know reflects the way we speak and not the independent nature of entities in the world.

To put all this more concisely: If our modal intuitions are to give us knowledge of the independent modal properties of things, it must be the case that we can focus (in thought) on a determinate entity (otherwise our question 'Is *x* necessarily *p*?' will be ambiguous, and there will be modal differences among the entities between which we are indeterminate which may be relevant to the question, as with 'Is water necessarily H_2O?'). But for any term *T* applied to an entity (set of entities) in the actual world, there will be more than one (indeed, infinitely many)[26] entities occupying the same space-time region, entities that may only be distinguishable by their modal features. To focus on any determinate one of them (for *T* to refer to any one of them), we need to separate it from the rest, and this can only be done by specifying how the thing is to be identified across possible worlds. But then, by the time we have focused on a determinate entity, we will already know what its modal properties are (under some description, for example, it may be as 'chemical microstructure' rather than 'H_2O' that one knows this necessary feature of water). It cannot be the case both that we are focused on a determinate individual (kind) *and* that we do not know (cannot find out *a priori*) what its modal properties are (under

[26]Of course, most of these will be quite peculiar entities, and it might be argued that their ontological status is such that we could not be referring to them unless we explicitly picked them out with a definite description. However, even if there is no threat from these entities of referential indeterminacy, there will always be entities of the more ordinary sort that must be distinguished if we are to make modal attributions about the referent of *T*, since they will differ in their modal features.

some description).[27] Thus, we do not come about modal knowledge by investigating a thing; the modal intuitions whereby we come about modal knowledge are reflections of how we have determined what it is that we are talking (thinking) about, and not of the thing thereby picked out. Again, considerations of the grounds upon which we assert necessities *a posteriori* support the view that these necessities are grounded in our conventions.[28]

More on Principles of Individuation[29]

We may notice that when we consider the sorts of referential intentions we should attribute to someone who thinks that Twin Earth 'water' is not water, we find something resembling general principles of individuation. In particular, the intention to refer to whatever is like *this* (glass of water) in respect of microstructure, or deepest causal features, creates the analytic context: $(x)(x$ is water $\supset x$ has the same microstructure as this).[30] When we add the empirical 'This is H_2O', we get the necessary *a posteriori* 'Water is H_2O'.

[27]This ties in with our earlier claim (chap. 3) that an expression cannot be both rigid and 'direct', or a 'mere tag'. Terms without some sort of sense cannot determinately refer to modally extended entities; the use of a term as a rigid designator does not, in any philosophically important way, allow us to conduct modal investigations the outcomes of which are not predetermined by our conventions.

[28]Notice that the above argument does not depend upon acceptance of my earlier claim that when a fully informed (about the actual world) Sly maintains that Twin Earth 'water' is water, we cannot (do not) simply say that he is wrong—although it does give us further reason to think that this is in fact the appropriate response.

[29]This section is of particular relevance to worries about the form and postulation of general principles of individuation, as presented in chapters 2 and 3.

[30]If this is not analytic, then we have not found the intention—we must consider what to say in various other possible circumstances. The point is that there is *some* intention, and whatever it is will create an analytic context of this sort.

This differs from our principles in generality, but it is compatible with my general view that all necessities *a posteriori* are derived from such particular analytic truths. However, as a point of psychological speculation, intentions of this particular sort would seem to be instances of a more general intention regarding, say, how to talk about natural kinds.[31] Thus, the intention regarding the use of 'water' is derivative from an intention that seems to create the following context: $(x)(x$ is a natural kind $\supset (y)(y$ belongs to $x \supset y$ has the same deep explanatory features as (most of) these samples of x (or, which we call 'x'))).

But this does not entail the principle about water: it does not follow from this that if water is H_2O, it is necessary that water is H_2O. Thus, if the more general intention is to explain what we say about Twin Earth, it must have the form: $(x)((x$ is a natural kind$) \supset \Box (y)(y$ belongs to $x \supset y$ has the same explanatory features as (most of) these samples of x)); or, if we want to talk about the kind, rather than its instances: $(x)((x$ is a natural kind$) \supset \Box (x$ has the same deep explanatory feature as (most of) these samples of x)), which is the same as our more familiar, $(x)((x$ is a natural kind$) \supset (P$ is the deepest explanatory feature of $x \supset \Box (x$ is $P)))$.

As formulated in chap. 2, then, the form of general principles of individuation can be seen as embodying the hypothesis that the referential intentions that set the stage for necessities *a posteriori* run in bunches, according to kinds more general than those for which we empirically find essences— our intentions regarding 'water' and the analytic context they create derive from a more general intention regarding the use of chemical compound terms, or even natural kind terms more generally, and which thus create similar contexts in-

---

[31]Putnam is in agreement here; the significant semantic inquiry is to be made into the notion of a 'natural kind word' rather than into, say, 'water' or 'lemon'. See his "Is Semantics Possible?" in *Philosophical Papers II: Mind, Language, and Reality* (Cambridge: Cambridge University Press, 1975c).

volving 'laughing gas', 'sulphuric acid', and 'sugar'. Note also that the modal operator occuring within the formalization of the convention is there for good reason: without it, we do not give an accurate account of the referential intention in virtue of which we deny that Twin Earth 'water' is water (this, of course, again on the assumption that our use of 'water' is derivative from a more general intention regarding terms that denote, say, chemical compounds or natural kinds). The peculiar form of general principles of individuation is not adopted for the purpose of allowing us to save, *ad hoc*, the empiricist conception of necessity, but because that form is needed to reflect the intentions with which we use certain sorts of words. If it is in fact false that we have these more general intentions, then the principles of individuation that explain the necessary *a posteriori* are not so general and so do not require that we represent them with a modal operator in their content; then, there would be lots of singular analytic contexts like '$(x)(x$ is water $\supset x$ has the same microstructure as this)', and the necessity of water's being H_2O would result not from a modal operator within the context, but from the context itself being governed by 'necessarily', as a result of its being analytic.

Thus, when we consider the basis upon which we assent to the necessity of *a posteriori* truths, we find not only that the necessity is convention-based, but we can also see what analytic truths our assent commits us to, that is, what conventions explain these necessities. Further, the claim that we have analytic principles of individuation is supported directly, and not just through our rejection of real necessity. The appeal to analytic (general) principles of individuation is not just a way of saving empiricism; it is the straightforward account of what goes on in our acceptance of the necessary *a posteriori*.

There is a further issue to be considered. Our conclusion to this point is that necessity, insofar as we have knowledge of it, is rooted in convention. This suffices to show that we do

have conventions of a certain sort, given that we have knowledge of necessity. But it might be wondered whether we
have positive reason to reject the claim that there *is* real necessity. Can we endorse the stronger thesis, that not only is
necessity convention-based insofar as we know of it, but that
this is all the necessity there is? I accept this stronger thesis
and shall try to defend it in the following section.

The Problem with Real Necessity: The Metaphysical Problem

It may be helpful if we continue along epistemological
lines for a moment. Suppose that there were real necessity.
Would it be possible for us to come to know such necessary
truths or essential predications? Certainly, we can imagine an
all-powerful being providing us with only true beliefs about
modal matters, but it will be more instructive to consider
whether we could arrive at such knowledge by rational
means, with no magical connections.

Our thinking about this question is constrained from two
sides. First, from the side of belief-formation, it is hard to get
away from thinking about how we actually come about
knowledge of necessity, that is, our reliance upon thought
experiments and imagination. We have already seen that
these methods can provide us with justification for beliefs
only about convention-based necessity, not real necessity.
But it is hard to see how we could be justified in our beliefs
about what is necessary *at all* without relying on such methods. If we cannot see what other methods could justify our
modal beliefs, then it would seem that the only kind of necessity of which we could have knowledge is convention-based
necessity. This points us toward considerations from another
side, the metaphysical side. Aside from our being influenced
by seeing how we actually justify modal claims, another reason why it is hard to see how we could come to have modal
knowledge by other means is because it is hard to see what
real necessity could be.

The bases for these two concerns are not unrelated. Epistemologically, the inability to tear ourselves away from the need for thought experiments or imaginative appeals stems from the fact that straight empirical methods seem adequate only for telling us what is actually the case. We need something extra to allow us to move to modal beliefs; we need, so to speak, some access to other possible worlds. Metaphysically, nothing in the actual world seems to be a candidate for determining what is necessarily the case. What is necessary depends on more than what is actual. To tie the points together, we cannot see how to justify modal beliefs other than as we do because we cannot see how modal reality could be determined other than by how we decide to speak (or think). To make sense of the (purely) empirical discovery of modality, we would have to be able to make sense of modality as an independent feature of the world. Our difficulty from the epistemological side provides some reason to think that we cannot make sense of such a notion.

But let us look at the metaphysical side of the issue in its own right. Here I do not really have any arguments besides: What could real necessity be? However, perhaps the force of this question could be focused.

Take a look around. Flowers are on the table. One flower is red. There is water in the glass. Music is playing. All these things can be imagined away. In a sense, one need merely look to see that these things do not have to be the case. Of course, these have never been candidates for necessary truths. But our intuitions are whetted. If a state of affairs is to be necessary, it must be somehow different from flowers being on the table. But how?

One way to come at this is to ask whether something could be added to the state of affairs comprised by the flowers being on the table in order to make it necessary. But this is certainly a dead end. The best we can do is to imagine that we have adopted a way of speaking such that flowers (or: what we there call 'flowers') are individuated by their location, so that if one imagines, as we would say, these flowers on the floor, one would have to say that what we imagine would not be these flowers. So if we are to make sense of a state of affairs differing from the flowers being on the table in such a way as to be necessary—as to be incapable of being imagined away—we must use a different approach. Necessity is not an 'ingredient' to be added to a state of affairs. There must be something about the state of affairs itself in virtue of which it is necessary, if there is to be real necessity. But it is hard to see what this could be. I think this sort of reflection on ordinary states of affairs gives rise to a strong suspicion that necessity is nothing in the world. This is not an argument, but a puzzlement: what, in what is actual, could make it the case that something could not be differently? In a way, since the intuition is not based on an argument, we are open to suggestion—'Show me'. But we have a strong suspicion that nothing that might be pointed to could change our minds.

The proper thing to do at this point is to consider some necessary truths. If we are going to see how something could be such that it cannot be imagined away, we should look at what is agreed to be necessary. Consider that bachelors are unmarried. We cannot imagine away that one. Can we find something in virtue of which this is necessary? We can, but it is not something to help us make sense of real necessity. What we find is that there is a linguistic rule in virtue of which 'bachelor' and 'never-been-married adult male' can be substituted for each other; 'unmarried' is part of the meaning of the term 'bachelor'. This is an important addition to the antinecessitarian intuition. For it seems that whenever we find something that cannot be imagined away, there is a convention in virtue of which this can be explained. This makes it reasonable to think that necessity has something to do with the way we speak (think), and not with the independent world.

It is also worth noting that the fact that bachelors are unmarried does not really present a picture that cannot be imagined away. It is not an 'immovable rock of reality'. For we can imagine individuals who are bachelors getting married, and we can imagine married men living quite as if they were bachelors—by themselves, dating often, no particular attachments, and so on. There is not any state of affairs—not even a general one—which we cannot imagine away. What we cannot do is describe things in a certain way.

It may be thought objectionable that I have chosen for my example a necessary truth that is analytic. However, my point holds for proposed necessities *a posteriori* as well; indeed, it holds especially for them. For if they could not be 'imagined away', they would be knowable *a priori*. So consider Margaret Truman's origin. Can we imagine away her being born of Harry and Bess? Well, we can picture someone living a life qualitatively identical to hers in every detail, except that she was born of a hospital cook and his wife and that she was mistakenly put in the 'Truman' incubator. But, if origin is essential, and Margaret *is* the child of Harry and Bess, then this woman could not be Margaret Truman. If I may gloss this in accordance with the above discussion, what this boils down to is that we are constrained not to *call* this woman 'Margaret Truman' (at least, not without creating ambiguity in the name).

When we think of something as a real essential property, we think of a special sort of tie between the property and its bearer, between, say, Margaret and her origin. If this were at root metaphysical, it seems, there should be some state of affairs that is impossible because of it. But it seems that, on the most straightforward understanding of 'state of affairs', true essential predications do *not* rule out any states of affairs. 'Margaret Truman was not born of Harry and Bess' is ruled out—but the sense in which this is true seems no different from that in which 'Some bachelors are married' is ruled out. In both cases, there are perfectly possible states of affairs that differ in no 'internal' respect from what is ruled out. All that seems to be really ruled out are certain ways of describing these states of affairs. But this seems to point up that in both cases—indeed, in all cases—the 'deep tie' is not given meta-physically but is a matter of how our linguistic conventions constrain our descriptions of situations.

Let me try to bring this point out another way. The idea is to think of states of affairs from the point of view of the world, so to speak. A metaphysical necessity would be a 'way the world must be'. But so long as we are thinking about ways the world could be, and not about how we can describe them, there does not seem to be any way the world cannot (or, thus, must) be; or, more pointedly, when we consider the best candidates for necessary truths, the 'ways the world might be' that would seem to have to be ruled out by these truths if they were *metaphysically* necessary are not ruled out. There may be no non-H_2O water, but there can be stuff that is just like water, and not H_2O. Considered non-verbally, this stuff is just what non-H_2O water would be. Water's necessarily being H_2O does not rule this out. What it rules out is this stuff's being water. But now I can make no other sense of this than that we will not call this stuff 'water'.

The intuition here is that if necessity were a real feature of the world, a real necessary truth would rule out some state of affairs, considered nonverbally. The fact that we need a description to explain what is ruled out shows that the necessity has a linguistic, and not a metaphysical, source. Thus, the consideration of necessary truths does not overturn the suspicion that there is no real necessity, but in fact supports it and the corresponding claim that necessity has its source in our conventions. Consideration of particular necessary truths gives us no clearer an idea of what real necessity could be than we got in considering things more abstractly. Indeed, it makes the question 'What could real necessity be?' look like the question 'What would pain be if it were a vegetable?' In trying to make sense of necessity as an independent feature of the world, we are looking in the wrong place.

Perhaps we can reformulate this. Take any synthetic necessity. There is no possible world in which it is false. However, we can imagine a situation that we would describe, if we were ignorant of certain actual facts, by a negation of the necessary proposition (or something that entails such a negation, as 'Water is H_3O' entails that it is not H_2O), even though, once our ignorance is cleared up, we will redescribe what we have imagined so as not to negate what is necessary. This has been called the 'epistemic possibility' of what is 'metaphysically impossible'. Wherever there is a synthetic necessary truth, there is an epistemically possible world that, while it is not metaphysically possible, is one in which that proposition is false.[32] There will also be a world that *is* metaphysically possible, in which the proposition is true, or at least, not false, that is qualitatively identical to this other metaphysically impossible world down to the smallest particle. But if the worlds are qualitatively identical, how can it be the case that only one of them is possible?

Indeed, one may wonder how it can be the case that these are different worlds at all. If this question has bite, and I think that it does, we must say either that what we have are two descriptions of the same situation, in which case the necessity is essentially linguistic rather than metaphysical, or that what makes these worlds different is that we have certain ways of describing or conceiving the world, in which case we still wind up with a linguistic account of the necessity. Either way, if we have the intuition that, speaking purely metaphysically, possible worlds that are qualitatively identical *are* identical, then the fact that there are worlds qualitatively identical to those in which synthetic necessities would be

[32]It may be objected that an 'epistemically possible but metaphysically impossible world' should not be called a world at all; it is rather a necessarily false description of what is actually metaphysically possible. Thus, there are not two qualitatively identical worlds, one possible and one not (see below), but *one* world and two descriptions—one correct and the other not. However, this objection seems to just make my point: necessary truths carry no metaphysical weight but merely represent constraints upon our linguistic behavior. In what follows, no important weight rests upon the 'world' description; what matters is just what difference there is supposed to be between what is and what is not possible.

false shows that these necessities are not metaphysical but result from our ways of conceiving the world.

Notice that I have not committed myself to the position that qualitatively identical worlds cannot be distinct, but only that, if they can be distinct, this must result from our ways of conceiving the world. I realize that even this (somewhat) weaker claim is controversial, but I do think it has a good deal of pull. Further, the challenge presented in the above argument does not even depend on this weaker claim, but on something weaker still, namely, that if two (epistemically) (possible) worlds are qualitatively identical, then if one of them is really metaphysically possible, then so must the other be. If only one of them is metaphysically possible, this must be a result of convention. Even if the stronger claim about the qualitative distinguishability of really distinct possible worlds can be reasonably challenged,[33] this weaker claim would stand as a force for real necessitarians to reckon with.

In this section I have tried to point to some of what gives rise to the anti-realist intuition concerning necessity. I think the intuition is strong and gives us good reason to accept a conventionalist view if one is available and compatible with the phenomena. But even if this overstates the case, we have independent epistemological considerations to support conventionalism about necessity. And I hope to have shown that this supports not merely conventionalism generally, but our conventionalist account in particular.

Partners in Crime?[34]

In this chapter, I have mostly been extolling the virtues of a conventionalist account of modality and more or less assert-

---

[33]For a lovely discussion of why we might want to avoid this claim, see Robert Adams, "Primitive Thisness and Primitive Identity," *Journal of Philosophy* 76 (1979): 5–26.

[34]This section was motivated by numerous discussions with David Brink and some offhand questions from Stephen Darwall.

ing that realists cannot answer the epistemological and metaphysical challenges I have raised. For the most part, this is simply because I do not see what options are available to the realist. However, there is one noteworthy move a realist about modality might make that merits response. The strategy I have used, it may be claimed, instantiates a familiar but generally suspicious line of argumentation that crops up in various areas of philosophy, particularly of recent note in metaethics. My argument mirrors a central sort of argument that is used against moral realism, and the modal realist may try to meet the challenge I have posed by means analogous to those that successfully salvage moral realism.

The moral anti-realist, or conventionalist, argument in question, like mine, has both an epistemological and metaphysical side.[35] Epistemologically, it asks 'How could we know these real, mind-independent moral truths?' and metaphysically, 'What could these moral facts or properties be?' The epistemological worry often starts from noting some sort of is/ought gap, from the claim that no moral conclusions can be inferred from wholly nonmoral premises. But how, then, are moral claims to be justified? It may seem that the only way out here is to suppose that we have some direct, noninferential access to moral reality, through some special faculty of intuition. But we have no reason to think that we have some such supernatural faculty. Even without focusing directly on is/ought worries, attention to our ordinary practice in moral reasoning displays our reliance upon moral intuitions, judgments about what is right or wrong in particular cases usually justified further, if at all, by intuitions about general moral principles, which themselves seem to stand outside the realm of further justification. But unless these intuitions come out of some peculiar faculty of moral perception or intuition, it is unclear what sort of access to a mind-independent moral reality they could afford us. This basic

---

[35]The now classical source for this argument is J. L. Mackie's *Ethics: Inventing Right and Wrong* (New York: Penguin Books, 1977).

worry may then be fueled by a metaphysical quandary about what moral facts or properties could be, and especially how they could fit into a naturalistic worldview. We know what it is for something to be square or six feet tall, but what is it for something to be *right*? This problem may seem especially acute if we focus on the action-guiding character of morality—what could make a fact essentially reason-giving, such that mere recognition of it has (desire-independent?) motivational force for an agent?[36] This metaphysical puzzle then filters back to a deeper epistemological concern—given how peculiar moral facts would need to be, it may look like not only our actual methods of moral inquiry are hard to understand as providing access to an independent moral reality, but that the only access we could have to such a reality, given its naturalistic surdness, would have to be through some mysterious, supernatural faculty in which we have no reason to believe. Thus, it has been argued, the only way to understand how there could be moral facts, and how our intuition-based methods could provide access to them, would be if these facts were somehow constituted, at least in part, by our cognitive activity, that is, by our moral intuitions.

This parallels much of the epistemological and metaphysical puzzles we have raised. We did not see how our reliance upon imagination and thought-experiments could provide access to a mind-independent modal reality. We said that it was hard to see what modal facts or properties could be— what it could be, in reality, that could make some fact not only hold, but hold necessarily, or could make some property essential. And we argued that we do not merely happen to depend upon imaginative appeals in our modal inquiry, but

[36]Though it isn't really relevant to the present discussion, I take it that there is ample reason to dismiss internalism as regards moral facts and motivation. See, for instance, Philippa Foot, "Morality as a System of Hypothetical Imperatives," *Philosophical Review* 81 (1972): 305–16, and David O. Brink, "Moral Realism and the Sceptical Arguments from Disagreement and Queerness," pp. 113–15.

that, given its outstripping of what is actual, it is hard to see what other methods could be adequate to modal knowledge. Our solution was that we could not make sense of a mind-independent modal reality, especially one that could be compatible with the modal knowledge we actually have, and to argue that, if we supposed that our conventions are partly constitutive of the modal facts, then we could understand both the facts and our knowledge of them. In both the moral and modal cases, then, we find a skeptical puzzle being raised and solved by a skeptical, or at least deflationary, solution.

There will be some to whom this parallel will not be at all troubling. On their view, these arguments against moral realism are compelling, so that the similarities cast no doubt upon the strength of our argument for conventionalism about modality. However, I am not among these thinkers. I do not think that the argument above gives us reason to reject moral realism or to accept some version of moral conventionalism. We will thus need to argue either that the arguments are not so parallel as they seem, or that the responses available to the moral realist are not available to the realist about necessity. Let me explain, then, why I think our argument succeeds where its metaethical counterpart fails.

It will be simplest to first see how the moral realist can successfully respond to the above argument.[37] First, the anti-realist argument smuggles in foundationalist epistemological assumptions. It supposes that our moral intuitions are supposed to have some sort of privileged epistemological position and to come, as it were, from nowhere, if not from a direct faculty of moral perception (intuition). However, the moral intuitions that figure in good moral inquiry need not and should not be considered as foundational. They represent our considered moral judgments and are to be justified, in the

---

[37]For a more detailed presentation, see David O. Brink, *Moral Realism and the Foundations of Ethics* (Cambridge: Cambridge University Press, 1989).

long run at least, by their presence in our best, most coherent, overall system of beliefs, both moral and nonmoral. The intuitions from which we start may be overturned,[38] and there is no need to postulate a special perceptual moral belief-forming faculty that must be explicable if our moral beliefs are to be justified or understood as giving us knowledge about a mind-independent reality. Our theory as a whole is about the world, our moral beliefs are part of that theory, and the theory is justified by its overall coherence, including explanatory power.[39] A rejection of foundationalism, then, forms the basis for a moral realist reply.

However, this would not, of itself, be sufficient if the moral realist could not say something naturalistically acceptable about the nature of moral facts and properties. Most simply, this is because naturalism is itself part of our best current total theory, and it is a constraint on acceptable belief that its objects be so explicable. Similarly, if we are to accept the output of particular belief-forming processes into our total theory, we must have grounds for thinking that these processes are conducive to the truth.[40] Thus, a coherentist or holist cannot merely say "Well, this is part of our best overall system of belief" and so needs no further justification. For a truth-conducive vindication of these processes is needed if their products *are* to be coherent with our overall system. More simply, perhaps, we need to note that in our current discussions about moral and modal realism, the beliefs we are

---

[38]See Rawls's discussion of reflective equilibrium, *A Theory of Justice* (Cambridge: Harvard University Press, 1971), pp. 20, 48–51.

[39]See Laurence Bonjour, *The Structure of Empirical Knowledge* (Cambridge: Harvard University Press, 1985), pt. 2.

[40]Seeing this as a central feature of a coherence theory of justification—indeed, as part of its argument against foundationalism—is one of the especially enlightening and admirable features of Laurence Bonjour's defense of coherentism. See "The Coherence Theory of Empirical Knowledge," *Philosophical Studies* 30 (1976): 281–312, and *The Structure of Empirical Knowledge*.

concerned with are not our particular moral and modal beliefs, but beliefs about the status of the reality that are the
truth-makers for these beliefs. And here it seems especially
clear that if realism in these cases is to be acceptable—
coherent with the rest of our beliefs—the moral or modal
facts must not step outside our naturalistic bounds, and we
must be in a position to understand how our means of justi-
fying these beliefs provides evidence of their truth.

It is here, in large part, that I think the moral and modal
cases diverge. The contemporary moral realist thinks that
moral facts supervene upon natural facts. The wrongness of
wanton torture consists in, is in some sense nothing over and
above, the gratuitous pain it causes its victim. The fact that
some instance of promise-breaking would frustrate the pro-
jects of another person realizes the fact that it shouldn't (to
that extent) be done. Moral properties don't float around as
something that must be added to a state of affairs to produce
their goodness or badness, but are right there in the natural
properties, in the way Russell's university is right there in its
buildings, students, faculty, and so on. And this being so, we
also do not need a special faculty of moral perception or
intuition to detect moral properties—all we need is our eyes
and ears. No doubt, moral perceptions can be produced only
with the help of moral background beliefs—they are theory-
laden and corrigible. But it is part of the rejection of foundationalism that this is true of all our (objectual) perceptual
beliefs and casts no special doubt on moral judgments.

Now, the problem of applying this response to the modal
case is that, short of our conventions and intentions, there is
nothing for modal properties or facts to supervene upon.
Necessity and contingency, essence and accident, outstrip the
actual. Nothing actual could suffice, in the way base properties must suffice for supervenient properties, for these modal
features. I have argued this already earlier (pp. 115–20),
and, indeed, it should be obvious. But consider, by way of

further illustration, the property of being a deepest explanatory feature—perhaps the most plausible candidate for a base
property for essentiality. What is it about properties of this
sort that makes them realize essentiality? We can say that
torture realizes badness because, say, it frustrates the flourishing of a person (sentient being), and personal (sentient)
flourishing is what goodness is. We can say that neural structure N realizes anger because it plays a certain functional role
and that that role defines anger. But there seems to be no
feature of H_2O that we can similarly say makes it realize
essentiality. Necessity isn't the property of being a deepest
explanatory feature in the way in which anger is the property
of filling a certain functional role. And this seems plain,
among other reasons, because the property of being a deepest
explanatory feature is a nonmodal property: it's an actual
property. If anything further is needed, we may also note
that not all deepest explanatory features are essential to their
objects/kinds, as we noticed earlier for water$_2$, which is only
accidentally H_2O, so that we lack here the upward determination needed for supervenience. Indeed, on reflection it
should be plain that the only feature common to all the sorts
of properties that realize essentiality, that is, that are essential
features of their objects/kinds, is their being chosen by us to
be individuating features. Without this, there is simply nothing about being a deep structure or any other sort of property
that could possibly suffice to make it essential. So the metaphysical escape hatch through which the moral realist can
preserve naturalistic acceptability, and thereby epistemological fecundity, is not available to the realist about necessity.
The metaphysical problem in the moral case involves either
overlooking certain options or the supposition that moral
facts would have to have properties that they do not, in fact,
require (see note 36); the only requirement that gives rise to
the metaphysical problem in the modal case is that necessary
properties be necessary—but that is quite enough.

There is another, deeper reason why the moral realist strat-

egy cannot be adopted by the modal realist. The moral realist, we saw, may claim that intuitions, as such, do not play
any special role in moral inquiry, but, rather, that what are
called 'intuitions' are just our considered moral judgments
culled from our overall theory. The realist about necessity
may then try to follow suit by claiming that it is not brute
appeals to imaginability or modal intuitions that have to provide the data for modal inquiry, but, rather, that our claims
about what would be true in various counterfactual situations
represent our considered modal beliefs, culled from our total
theory. It is thus inappropriate to focus on imaginative appeals and to ask what access they in particular give us to a
mind-independent modal reality; rather, the question of access should be asked only of our total evidentiary system.

However, for the reasons discussed above in the section
called "In Addition," this move cannot be made successfully
in the modal case. As we saw there, we cannot make out the
claim that our judgment, for instance, that the liquid on
Twin Earth is not water simply represents our considered
beliefs about the essential features of water. This was because
antecedent to a judgment about whether that stuff is water,
or some modal judgment that entailed it, there could be
nothing to determine whether 'water' in our idiolect (or system of mental representation) referred to water or water$_2$,
and consequently, no basis for judging either that 'This Twin
Earth stuff is (would be) water' is true or that it is false: there
would simply be no unique proposition expressed, and no
uniformity of truth value among those among which the
sentence is ambiguous. One's beliefs cannot be about water,
rather than water$_2$, until one has antecedently determined, at
least through a general principle, that the individuating feature that guides the reference of 'water' is microstructure, or
causal depth. Our reports on counterfactual cases, then, cannot be said to simply represent our considered beliefs about
the entities in question because our beliefs cannot be about
those entities unless we have already determined, at least by

implication, what our judgments are to be in these counter-factual cases. But this is to say that these reports cannot properly be thought of, in the first instance, as 'beliefs' proper at all, but as stipulations or consequences thereof.

Perhaps a slightly different way of putting the point is to say that since it is what is true of a thing in counterfactual situations that determines what it *is*, and so that representation of a thing requires determination of its essential features, modal judgments—or at least some of them (the basic ones)—*are* foundational: there is no inquiry that can support them because they are presupposed by any determinate inquiry. But there is no mystery here about how this can be, for this special status comes from the fact that these are not empirical judgments at all, but are analytic products of individuating decisions.

It will be noticed that no similar problem arises for the moral realist who wishes to represent our intuitions as considered moral beliefs. This is because we can easily focus on or refer to an action or state of affairs in ways that are independent of and do not presuppose moral judgments. This is no surprise. It is peculiar to modal inquiry, because of the individuating nature of modal properties, that we must somehow determine our answers before there can be a determinate subject for our inquiry to be about. It is this special feature of modal inquiry, of the relation between modality and representation, which I think gives the epistemological arguments we have considered in this chapter special purchase and renders them crucially disanalogous from other skeptical arguments.

Whatever structural similarity, then, that there may be between the arguments I have presented and probably unsuccessful arguments against moral realism and for a sort of moral conventionalism, I believe that considerations particular to the content of modality and the investigation of modality prevent the realist about necessity from satisfactorily offering responses parallel to those of moral realists. The arguments cannot be dismissed as presupposing an illegitimate foundationalism, nor can the realist easily hope to discharge his duty to offer a naturalistically acceptable account of either the metaphysics or the epistemology of modality.

The Causal Theory?

It may finally be objected that I have failed to take into account the causal theory of reference. Since it is in discussions of such theories that the necessary *a posteriori* was originally advocated, one might think that we cannot fairly evaluate the status of these modal truths without considering the theory of reference and how it is related to them. In chapter 6, I will discuss the relation between essentialism and the causal theory of reference. However, the above objection can be met without getting very involved in such a discussion.

For one thing, while we have not considered the causal theory itself, we have considered arguments that have occurred within the context of discussions of the theory, and have seen that they do not support realism. In addition, we have considered the causal theory indirectly in our discussion of how we come to know that water is necessarily H_2O. For the picture suggested by the causal theory is that, by virtue of causal connections alone, we achieve reference to some individual or kind in the actual world and can then conduct modal inquiries about that to which we have referred. Of course, on that picture, the causal theory does not support realism against our objections, for it does not suggest anything we have not already considered about how we come to know modal truths. But we argued further that in order for the determinate reference required for such inquiries to take place, there must be some element of intention involved in order to make it the case that we refer to one rather than another of the overlapping entities or coextensive kinds that stand in identical causal relations to us and to our uses of terms. This element of intention not only compromises the causal theory in the direction of empiricist semantics (see chapters 3 and 6), but shows further that, insofar as the causal theory is relevant to the issue of modal realism, it does not offer any support for the realist position and supports, if anything, conventionalism.

Finally, it may be suggested that there is a different picture suggested by the causal theory: We refer to some actual individual (kind) rigidly, and our knowledge of this rigidity, plus actual features of the world, allows us to gain modal knowledge. On this view, essentialism is derived from the causal theory of reference, plus modally uninteresting empirical facts. Nathan Salmon has argued that this is false,[41] that the derivations implicitly smuggle in nontrivial essentialist claims that are no part of the theory of reference. If this is true, then the above picture is faulty and inadequate to our modal knowledge. However, even if Salmon is wrong (see chapter 6), the very fact of the derivation should show us that the derived modal truths are of no great metaphysical interest. Deductive consequences contain nothing not found in their premises, and, as there is nothing metaphysically deep (modally) either in a theory of reference or, by definition, modally uninteresting empirical facts, necessary truths that resulted from them could hardly be thought to carry any metaphysical weight. It would just be that somehow our way of setting up the relation of reference determined how we carry the actual over into the possible—which is what conventionalists have been claiming all along. Either way, then, the causal theory of reference does not offer any additional support, beyond providing for the possibility of necessary truths *a posteriori*, for realism about necessity.

Conclusion and Prelude: The Commitment to Analyticity

I hope to have provided some reason to think that we have no notion of what real necessity could be, or at least to have

---

[41]Nathan Salmon, *Reference and Essence* and "How *Not* to Derive Essentialism from the Theory of Reference."

conveyed the intuition that there is no real necessity. Even if I have not, however, adequately supported a general skepticism here, I believe that the epistemological considerations adduced above show that what necessity we do have knowledge of is convention-based, and that if we have knowledge of necessary truths that cannot be known *a priori*, these truths owe their modal status to our linguistic conventions. This being so, we have reason to think that there are (general) principles of individuation that are analytic.

This conclusion may be discomforting. Have we not by now learned that the notion of analyticity is suspect, or, at least, that if there are any analytic truths, they are few and unimportant? It might be thought that if we are committed to systematically important analytic truths, we are in deep trouble. One may be so suspicious of analytic truths that one would rather postulate real necessity. I hope that the above disussion has shown this to be an unsatisfactory alternative. If one is completely unwilling to countenance analytic truths of the sort I am proposing, one ought to reject the necessary *a posteriori*. It is the acceptance of such truths that commits us to either real necessity or analytic principles of individuation; if both of these are unacceptable, we must reject the premise that has forced us to choose between them.

Furthermore, it is by considering these very truths that we are led to think that we have analytic general principles. It is not simply that necessary truths *a posteriori* commit us to analytic general principles if we are unwilling to recognize real necessity; rather, investigating the truths themselves supports directly the claim to analyticity. For when we consider the basis upon which we assent to the necessary *a posteriori*, we find appeals to imagination and *a priori* considerations that can only be understood to give us insight into our conventions. Thus, we ought to believe, independently of a general skepticism about real necessity, that if we have knowledge of necessary *a posteriori* truths, then we have analytic general principles of individuation, and that if this analyticity is too hard to swallow, we should reject the claims of necessities *a posteriori*.

My general claim, then, that if we accept the necessary *a posteriori*, we should accept analytic general principles of individuation in virtue of which their necessity is explained, still stands even if we do have reason to reject this sort of analyticity, and so, then, does my defense of conventionalism against a realism motivated by the necessary *a posteriori*. However, if we find the arguments on behalf of the necessary *a posteriori* plausible, then since they so directly support the claim that we have analytic general principles of individuation, we should not be so unwilling to admit that we have such principles. They are a straightforward postulate in virtue of which we can explain why we make the judgments we do regarding these proposed necessities. Rejecting this postulate forces us not merely to reject the necessary *a posteriori*, but leaves us at a loss to explain hard empirical data, namely, the fact that we judge these truths to be necessary, that we make the judgments that lead to this conclusion. But it will perhaps be easier to soften anti-analyticity sentiments by discussing the subject more directly. This is the matter of the next chapter.

5 The Commitment to Analyticity

IN THE LAST CHAPTER, I argued that if we think there are necessary truths *a posteriori*, then we should think there are analytic general principles of individuation. A concern over appeals to analyticity was noted, but we saw that this does not threaten the empiricist account offered: if one cannot accept analytic general principles, then one should reject the necessary *a posteriori*. However, I do not think such a rejection would be warranted. It is the central claim of this chapter that the fact that necessary truths *a posteriori* commit us to analytic principles of individuation gives us no reason to deny that there are such truths if we are otherwise so persuaded.

I first defend the claim that our support for general skepticism about analyticity is not so great as to override good independent reason to accept the necessary *a posteriori*. This concludes the central argument for and defense of my thesis about necessity and analyticity. However, I also argue that we are committed to analytic principles of individuation whatever we think about the necessary *a posteriori*. If this is so, then clearly the fact that accepting necessities *a posteriori* commits us to such principles can give us no reason not to accept these necessities. In addition, if we do have such independent commitment to analytic principles, this is of quite independent interest, as will be apparent to anyone familiar with the prevalent anti-analyticity sentiment of the past thirty-five years.[1] Thus, my central claim is that the commitment to analytic general principles of individuation should not scare us away from the necessary *a posteriori*;[2] and by way of defending this (though it is not at all essential to the defense), I shall also argue for the more substantive claim that, empirical necessities or no, there *are* analytic principles of individuation.

Part 1. Why the Commitment to Analyticity Cannot Make Us Reject the Necessary *A Posteriori*

1. *Analyticity versus Real Necessity*

I claimed earlier that if we find analyticity too difficult to bear, then the proper response is not to reject my account of empirical necessities, but to deny that there are any such empirical necessities. I am assuming that the argument in chapter 4 provided good reason to accept the view that if there are necessary truths *a posteriori*, then there are analytic general principles of individuation (in virtue of which the

---

[1]Some of the more famous anti-analyticity literature: W. V. O. Quine, "Two Dogmas of Empiricism," in *From a Logical Point of View*; "Truth by Convention," in *The Ways of Paradox*; *Word and Object* (Cambridge: MIT Press, 1960), sec. 14; Hilary Putnam, "The Analytic and the Synthetic," "Is Semantics Possible?" "The Meaning of 'Meaning'," all in *Mind, Language and Reality*; Morton White, "The Analytic and the Synthetic," in Leonard Linsky, ed., *Semantics and the Philosophy of Language* (Urbana: University of Illinois Press, 1952).

[2]This may be thought a peculiar sort of claim to defend—wouldn't the more natural line for an opponent of analyticity to take be to suggest that the rejection of analyticity gives us reason to deny my claim that the necessary *a posteriori* commits us to analytic principles of individuation? While this is, perhaps, the more appropriate first response, I am supposing that it is no longer a live option after the discussion of chapter 4. However, see also the discussion of the next section.

modal feature of these truths is to be explained). During those arguments, I tried to show that real necessity would be quite mysterious, metaphysically and epistemologically. Thus, if we reject the explanation of necessity by reference to our conventions, then we are committing ourselves to something quite occult. Analyticity, however, is not so mysterious. We may have good reasons to think there is none, but among these is not the occult to which we would have to resort. We know what it is to intend to refer, and we have some idea of what coordinated intentions are. We may think that we can do our semantics without talking about such things, but if we cannot, we are not thereby thrust upon magic. Thus, analyticity is easier to live with than real necessity.

The point of this is as follows. Quite often, when a combination of beliefs—a conditional and its antecedent—entails the falsity of a well-confirmed generalization, we will reject the conditional. The conditional will typically be supported by the claim that the consequent provides the best explanation for the truth of the antecedent. But if the consequent's truth would establish the falsity of a well-confirmed generalization, we are inclined to reject the conditional or, more specifically, the claim that the consequent provides the best explanation of the antecedent. Thus, if a vase unexpectedly falls over and someone says (sincerely) 'There are evil forces in this house,' our well-confirmed belief that there are no such forces will support our confidence that there must be some other explanation—we reject the conditional (that is, that if an object falls over for no apparent reason, then it was knocked over by evil forces).

Now, the point of my talk, a paragraph back, of the relative occultness of real necessity and analyticity was to show that the above strategy is inapplicable in our case. Given our strong background reason to reject the occult, we cannot appeal to our disbelief in analyticity to demand another explanation of necessities *a posteriori*. The cost of postulating real necessity removes this as an option; 'There must be some explanation other than analyticity' will not do. Forced to choose between analyticity and real necessity, we must choose the former. However bad analyticity may be, real necessity is worse. Thus, again, opponents of analyticity may try to argue, if they wish, that since the necessary *a posteriori* commits us to analyticity, we should deny that there are any such necessary truths, and it is in response to such argument that this chapter is written. However, the above considerations have been designed to show what I hope was already clear, that it is not open to those philosophers to appeal to the problems with analyticity to reject my account, and so to commit themselves to real necessity. Let us move on, then, to consider how seriously we should worry about the commitment to analyticity.

2. Worries about Analyticity: Part 1

I believe that there are three basic sources for the scorn, suspicion, and smirks with which talk about analyticity is commonly met in much of the contemporary philosophical community:

(1) Quine's arguments in "Two Dogmas of Empiricism" and elsewhere, both as they stand, and as elaborated by Putnam;

(2) success in finding counterexamples to many proposed or plausibly analytic statements, along with a general failure to find analytic definitions for most English words; and

(3) the development of causal theories of reference, according to which reference occurs without the aid of definitions for terms, thus rendering analytic connections superfluous.

Our question is whether any of these provides enough support for disbelief in analyticity to overturn good independent reason to accept the claim that there are necessary truths *a posteriori* (and, therefore, analytic general principles of individuation).

It is plain to see that grounds (2) and (3) cannot provide such support by themselves. Consider (2). We may agree that most proposed analytic truths are not in fact analytic and, further, that analytic definitions do not seem to be forthcoming for most terms. Indeed, this is to be expected if we have analytic general principles. They govern the semantics for kinds of terms and make it the case that the extensions of these (subsumed) terms will be set empirically. Now, suppose we accept that there are necessary truths *a posteriori* and come to believe that this commits us to there being analytic principles. Do the above considerations give us reason to doubt the necessary *a posteriori*? If it is true that there are such truths, then there will be some truths to which we cannot produce conceivable counterinstances.[3] But the induction from 'We have always found counterexamples' to 'We will always be able to find counterexamples' depends in part upon our having no independent reasons to think that there are analytic truths. And the necessary *a posteriori* gives us such independent reason. Without theoretical support, straight inductions cannot justify rejecting claims that would establish counterinstances—at least, not if those claims have good support. Indeed, it is not even clear that without theoretical support such inductions are justified at all.[4] At any rate, the firmness of straight inductions can extend no further than good reason to accept counterinstances, and they can carry no weight as far as rejecting those grounds is concerned. Put another way, the argument: (1) We have always been able to

---

[3]These will be, of course, the analytic principles, not the necessary *a posteriori* truths. The *a posteriority* of the latter ensures that there *will* be conceivable, or 'apparently conceivable' (though not possible), counterexamples for them.

[4]This suspicion is at least as old as Hume's *Enquiry* and receives some of its classical formulation in Nelson Goodman's "The New Riddle of Induction" and "The Problem of Counterfactual Conditionals," both in *Fact, Fiction and Forecast* (Indianapolis: Bobbs-Merrill, 1965).

find counterexamples; (2) If there are necessary truths *a posteriori*, we will not always be able to do so; therefore (3) there are no such necessary truths, constitutes straightforward question-begging, unless we have independent reason to think that there are theoretical grounds for our always being able to find counterexamples. But if there is any such reason, it is not to be found in grounds (2) alone.

However, it seems fair to say anyway that success in finding counterexamples to proposed analytic truths has played but a supplementary role in the general rejection of analyticity: it backs up Quine's more general reasons for thinking that all (interesting) statements are revisable.

Grounds (3) above may seem to provide some more theoretical support for the rejection of analyticity. There are, however, two shortcomings here. The first is that in order to justify a general suspicion of analyticity, we would have to have grounds for thinking that causal theories of reference provide an adequate account of reference for all terms. However, even if we do have reason to accept a causal theory of reference for natural kind terms and proper names—something that is still quite up in the air, at least in the former case—no one has made it plausible that this can be extended completely generally. Thus, suspicion of analyticity here can extend only as far as it is reasonable to think a causal theory can extend satisfactorily.

Now, it might be claimed that for present purposes, at least, the causal theory extends far enough, since our concern is here (largely) with individual names and natural kind terms. But this is not obvious. We are not claiming analyticity for sentences beginning with 'water', 'sulphur', or 'tigers', but rather those with, say, 'chemical compounds', 'biological species', or even more generally 'natural kinds' as subject terms. And it is not completely clear, especially in this last case, that these are natural kind terms.

This is related to the second and far more important shortcoming of the 'argument from the causal theory' (that is, (3)).

Suppose we grant full generality to the causal theory or at least grant that the subject terms (for example, 'chemical compounds') are natural kind words. It is still not obvious that, as grounds (3) claims, the causal theory of reference renders analyticity superfluous. As I argue both later in this chapter and in chapter 6, I think that, insofar as a causal theory of reference is plausible at all, analytic general principles of individuation play an important role in the determination of reference. Not to give the whole argument now, we might just notice this. The causal theory of reference and the necessary *a posteriori* go hand in hand. It is no accident that the latter is presented and argued for in discussion of the former. Once we are free from the bonds of analytic definitions for all terms, we are free to discover the features constraining the modal identification of individuals and kinds. The causal theory of reference is supposed to show, among other things, how it could be sensible to talk about real essences rather than merely nominal ones. The causal theory falls within a general realist project, part of which is to show that our science gets at a real, independent structure of the world, and that (apparent) changes in belief about even the most fundamental features of things may represent our coming to know better the true nature of these things rather than our simply adopting new conventions. We discover, not stipulate, the essences of the things we talk about. So it is hard to see how we could use the causal theory of reference to argue that there are no necessary truths *a posteriori*, even if these commit us to some analyticity. *Some* analyticity is compatible with *very little* analyticity, and there is nothing within the causal theory to make us think there cannot be *any*. In particular, accepting some analytic general principles of individuation is compatible with denying that there are any analytic definitions for particular natural kind terms, and it is these that are the central target of the causal theory. On the other hand, asserting that there are no necessary truths *a posteriori*, while possibly compatible with the causal theory (again, I argue in chapter 6 that it is not), undercuts a fundamental motivation for that theory. Causal theorists should give up such necessity only very grudgingly—more grudgingly, I think, than they should accept a few analytic principles of individuation. Thus, the causal theory is committed to analyticity either directly, or indirectly through the necessary *a posteriori*, and so cannot provide a fully general support for the rejection of analyticity. And, most obviously, it cannot provide the sort of support for that rejection in virtue of which we could reject the necessary *a posteriori*, for, again, such necessities are central to the very program of which the causal theory is a part.

Thus, neither the causal theory of reference nor the success we have had in finding counterexamples to proposed analytic truths give us so much reason to reject significant analyticity that we ought to reject necessary truths *a posteriori* even if we have good reason to accept them. If we are to find such reason to reject the necessary *a posteriori*, then, it must reside in Quine's considerations against analyticity (grounds (1) above). It is to these considerations we now turn.

3. Worries, Part 2: Quine and "Two Dogmas of Empiricism"

In the first four sections of "Two Dogmas," Quine considers a family of concepts with which we might try to define, or explicate, the notion of analyticity. In each case, he finds that the defining notion is either itself no more clear than the notion of analyticity, or itself requires explanation in terms of analyticity. Any plausible-looking definition of 'analyticity', then, is either unclear or circular, and the status of 'analyticity' is thus at best murky.

This argument has not been taken to have a great deal of force, and it is not that in virtue of which "Two Dogmas" has had its great philosophical impact. Mates[5] and Grice and

[5]Benson Mates, "Analytic Sentences," *Philosophical Review* 60 (1951): 525–34.

Strawson[6] argue that the sort of circularity to which Quine points need not be vicious and that we may improve our understanding of 'is analytic' by paying attention to some of these 'definitions'.[7] Further, the restrictions that Quine places upon what is to count as a satisfactory definition are too strong by any reasonable standard and would rule out a great deal beyond 'analyticity' if adhered to generally. Thus, Grice and Strawson: "We may well begin to feel that a satisfactory explanation is hard to come by. . . . It is perhaps dubious whether *any* such explanations can *ever* be given. . . . [I]t would be pretty generally agreed that there are . . . cases in which they cannot" (p. 148). It is also worth noting that a great majority of those who oppose significant analyticity will grant at least trivial cases—'Bachelors are unmarried', 'A vixen is a female fox', 'If one object is larger than another, the second is smaller than the first'. They thus cannot think that

---

[6]H. P. Grice and P. F. Strawson, "In Defense of a Dogma," *Philosophical Review* 65 (1956): 141–58.

[7]Though I do not wish to defend this as a definition of 'analyticity', I do not think that Quine's rejection of interchangeability in all contexts (sec. 3) is satisfactory. He says correctly that, in a purely extensional language, interchangeability will not do as a criterion of analyticity, and then remarks that while substitutivity in contexts governed by 'necessarily' will get us something at least coextensive with analyticity, we understand 'is necessary' only insofar as we understand 'is analytic' (p. 31). But we do not need 'necessarily' in order to get into an intensional language—verbs of propositional attitude will do quite well. Now, Quine certainly has worries about intensional languages of any sort, and not only those made intensional by modal idioms. However, the particular charge he levies here is that of circularity, or, more exactly, 'closed curvature in space' (p. 30), and it is far from clear that we understand 'believes' and 'desires' only insofar as we antecedently understand the notion of analyticity. So if there is circularity in an appeal to substitutivity in all, including intensional, contexts—now that we see we do not need to make use of 'necessarily' as our intensional expression—more needs to be said to convince us. Again, there may be other arguments against intensionality generally, but at least many who have followed Quine concerning analyticity are not inclined to give up verbs of propositional attitude, and if they can give us a foothold on analyticity, it's so much the better for analyticity—not so much the worse for belief and desire.

no good sense can be made of the notion of analyticity. It must be, then, that they find other considerations telling against significant analytic truths; insofar as these come from Quine, they reside in his other arguments. And even those few who are so bold as to deny the analyticity of, say, 'Bachelors are unmarried' do not seem to do so on the grounds that they do not understand the claim that the sentence is analytic. Rather, they claim to have conceivable (or actual) counterinstances.[8] Between this evidence and the apparent weakness of the argument, I think that we can conclude that sections 1–4 of "Two Dogmas" are not the source of much suspicion of analyticity. I should like to add a quote from Putnam, both for its concise criticism and as a testimony against this argument of Quine's as the actual source of the influence of "Two Dogmas":

> At a superficial level . . . Quine is going to show us that there is no sense to be made of the notion of analyticity by showing that all of the suggested definitions lead in circles. But (as Grice and Strawson long ago pointed out) it is puzzling why this is supposed to be a good argument. Could it not, after all, just be the case that the various members of the family of linguistic notions to which the notion of analyticity belongs are not definable in terms of, or reducible to other, non-linguistic notions? . . . Something more doubtless needs to be said about the status of such linguistic notions . . . but a mere demonstration of definitional circularity would hardly seem to be enough to overthrow as widely accepted and used a notion as the notion of analyticity.[9]

The important action, then, both philosophically and in producing the suspicion of analyticity so prevalent today,

---

[8]See, for example, Gilbert Harman, *Thought* (Princeton: Princeton University Press, 1973), p. 105, for some quite cavalier claims in this regard.

[9]Hilary Putnam, "Two Dogmas Revisited," in *Philosophical Papers III: Realism and Reason* (Cambridge: Cambridge University Press, 1983), p. 88.

must occur in sections 5 and 6 of "Two Dogmas," in Quine's reflections upon the holistic nature of our belief systems—the manner in which our beliefs confront "the tribunal of sense experience not individually but only as a corporate body" ("Two Dogmas," p. 41). No particular experience, or set of experiences, guarantees the truth of any particular statement or belief (except perhaps the statement that we have had these experiences—and even this is problematic, insofar as reports of sense experience carry with them judgments of similarity),[10] and, further, we can imagine ourselves, for any such set of experiences, to be in an epistemic situation such that the best thing for us to do is to reject what would seem to be the straightforward report suggested by these experiences (for example, 'There is a table before me').

> Total science is like a field of force whose boundary conditions are experience. A conflict with experience at the periphery occasions readjustment in the interior of the field . . . Reevaluation of some statements entails reevaluation of others, because of their logical interconnections . . . [T]he total field is so underdetermined by its boundary conditions, experience, that there is much latitude of choice as to what statements to reevaluate in the light of any single experience. ("Two Dogmas of Empiricism," p. 42)

Similarly, because of this unity and interdependence of belief, any statement we accept is a potential candidate for revision. Since any belief may belong (essentially) to a set of beliefs of which we must reject at least one member,[11] there is no guarantee that we shall never find it most satisfactory to reject that belief.

---

[10]See especially Wilfred Sellars, "Empiricism and the Philosophy of Mind," in H. Feigl and M. Scriven, eds., *Minnesota Studies in the Philosophy of Science*, vol. 1 (Minneapolis: University of Minnesota Press, 1956).

[11]The 'essentially' here is meant to signify that if we were to subtract the statement in question, we would not be required to modify the resultant set of beliefs.

This may seem like a purely logical point, that, insofar as any statement can belong to an inconsistent set of claims each of which we are inclined (indeed, have good reason) to believe, for all logic tells us, any statement could be given up to resolve the conflict.[12] However, Quine's point is stronger. It is that for any statement, it may be reasonable, under possible epistemological circumstances, for us to give up that statement. This stronger claim, which must be true if Quine is to really have an argument against analyticity here, is supported by episodes in the history of science. Basic principles, which have appeared to many of those who believed them to be definitions, linguistic stipulations, and thus immune from revision, have been repeatedly given up in the history of science. Because they were so fundamental, it seemed that their negations were literally unimaginable. But we now know them to be not only imaginable, but also true. So why should we think now, even of statements whose negations seem impossible, that anything we believe is actually analytic and unrevisable? So long as a statement belongs to the web of belief, it must be seen as potentially up for grabs.

> No statement is immune from revision. Revision of even the logical law of excluded middle has been proposed as a means of simplifying quantum mechanics, and what difference is there in principle between such a shift and the shift whereby Kepler superseded Ptolemy, or Einstein Newton, or Darwin Aristotle? ("Two Dogmas of Empiricism," p. 43)

Thus, Quine provides us with both inductive and theoretical reasons for thinking that there are no analytic truths. The theoretical reasons stem from his epistemological holism—

---

[12]By 'logic' here, I mean 'straight logic', i.e., the sentential and quantificational calculi plus identity. I do *not* mean to include what may be part of logic more broadly construed, i.e., meaning postulates or analytic connections. Obviously, if these were included, then even the weak claim that 'for all logic tells us, any belief could be given up' would beg the question.

his insight that our beliefs form a 'field of force,' a web whose parts do not confront experience piecemeal—and the inductive reasons from the history of science support what this holism should lead us to expect, that no part, that is, no particular statement, is completely immune from the possibility of revision. We may now ask whether the argument supports the rejection of analyticity strongly enough to override good independent reason to accept necessary truths *a posteriori*.

We may first consider a response to Quine's general argument suggested by Grice and Strawson. They claim that our belief in the analytic/synthetic distinction is conclusively supported by our ability to classify sentences as belonging to these categories with respect to an open class of sentences.[13] Now, this may conclusively support the view that there is an actual distinction demarcated by our terms 'analytic' and 'synthetic': it does nothing, however, to show that this distinction is the one we think it is.[14] It does not show, in particular, that necessarily true, *a priori*, and unrevisable statements fall onto one side of the schism, and conceptually contingent, empirical statements onto the other. In fact, this response plays right into Quine's hands. He wishes to acknowledge a real distinction—that between statements closer to the center of our 'total theory' and those closer to the periphery. Indeed, this is an essential part of Quine's argument. For there is a real phenomenon that motivates belief in the analytic/synthetic distinction and the belief that analytic sentences are unrevisable. This is the apparent inability to imagine the falsity of some of the statements we accept, and the sense that the negations of some statements are not just obviously or wildly false, but nonsensical.[15] Quine must be

---

[13]Grice and Strawson, "In Defense of a Dogma," p. 143.

[14]Grice and Strawson acknowledge this; for them, as for me here, this is but a preliminary point by way of opening the discussion. See pp. 143ff.

[15]Grice and Strawson, pp. 32–33.

able to explain this if he is to succeed in his project. And as we have just noted, he has an explanation. Some beliefs are central to our total theory; they are presupposed or taken for granted in a great many of our epistemic activities. It is thus difficult to imagine, in a simple way, experiences that could make us give up such central beliefs—for it is always easier to give up something else. To put the point slightly differently, a situation in which central statements are false would have to be one in which so many of our other beliefs are false that it is extremely difficult to go about imagining such a situation. This is why it is sometimes said that while all beliefs are revisable, some could be given up only as parts of a wholesale abandoned theory. Thus, Quine can explain, in terms of theoretical centrality, the apparent unrevisability of certain of our beliefs in virtue of which we first come to the analytic/synthetic distinction. And, by the same token, he can acknowledge that there is a real distinction we are getting at. But this distinction is not a very deep one—it is only that between statements closer to and further away from the center of the web of belief. This is not a difference in kind. Insofar as we think of analyticity as involving or entailing real unrevisability, we ought not to believe that there are analytic truths.

But Quine's explanation of the apparent inability to imagine the falsity of some statements is not wholly adequate. For many statements that we believe to be analytic on these grounds are not at all theoretically central. That bachelors are unmarried or that vixen are female foxes, do not seem to be deeply intertwined with much else we believe. These truths are not presupposed in a great deal of our everyday or scientific reasoning. Certainly, they do have connections with other beliefs of ours, and there are sets of inconsistent beliefs we can have to which they can (essentially) belong. But this makes them neither central nor revisable. Consequently, our belief in their unrevisability cannot be explained by their centrality; such belief must have some other source.[16] And the most plausible candidate is that these statements *are* unrevisable and are so because they are analytic. This is enough, I think, to save the analytic/synthetic distinction in basically its traditional form, that is, analyticity entails *a prioricity* and full-scale unrevisability; some statements are true quite independently of the way the world happens to be, because their truth is not a matter of fact, but rather a product of our linguistic conventions.

But this is hardly adequate as a complete response to Quine and will certainly not support the necessary *a posteriori* against those who think that we cannot accept what will commit us to analyticity. For even if they must grant that there are some genuinely analytic truths, they may claim that there are none of any interest. Indeed, we noted earlier that most foes of analyticity do grant the typical, trivial examples. The modified form of Quine's thesis that they accept, and justify largely by Quine's considerations (supplemented by grounds (2) and (3); see p. 136), is this: There are no important, or interesting, or philosophically significant analytic truths. As Putnam puts it, " 'Chair' may be synonymous with 'movable seat for one with a back' but that bakes no philosophical bread and washes no philosophical windows."[17] I assume that all this is pertinent to our case for at least two reasons: First, analytic principles of individuation are being put forth for the very purpose of washing some philosophical windows, namely, explaining how there can be and how we can know necessary *a posteriori* truths. Second, insofar as these analytic principles govern the use of natural kind terms and individual names, I would think that they would be of some

---

[16]Conversely, there are many 'central' beliefs which do not seem at all analytic, or the negations of which seem unimaginable, e.g., 'Evolution proceeds by random mutation.'

[17]"The Analytic and the Synthetic," p. 36.

philosophical interest. So, we are now interested in considering Quine's argument viewed as supporting the modified and more commonly accepted Quinean claim, that there are no interesting analytic truths.

Modifying the argument is a simple matter: What makes a statement interesting is its theoretical centrality, the degree of its connections with and implications for other statements we accept. If we knew that force equaled acceleration times mass, that would be important. If we knew that something with two legs was biped or that "Green Acres" was on television after "Gilligan's Island," there would be nothing of great significance to be learned in consequence. However, and here we return to Quine, theoretical centrality is sufficient for revisability in principle. If a belief has many connections with others, then things could conceivably become discordant enough that we found it reasonable—or, as Quine might say, most economical—to give up that central belief. More generally, a theoretically central belief is part of a theory. In a theory that, as a whole, is about some portion of the world, there can be no separation of the component statements into those that are empirical and those that are linguistic. It is always possible that we shall someday find it reasonable to adopt a new theory. We try, of course, in later theories to preserve what was correct in the earlier ones, typically by showing earlier central claims to be approximately, but not exactly, true. But there is no guarantee (and, indeed, there is good reason to doubt) that any one statement of an overthrown theory will survive unscathed.

To sum up, in order for a statement to be interesting, it must have significant interconnections with other statements we accept. But if it is so interconnected, we cannot rule out the possibility of its rational revision. Thus, while there may be some analytic truths, there cannot be any interesting ones.

But the modified argument, while for a weaker conclusion, is not, I think, as strong as the original. For in granting, as it must, that there are some genuine analytic truths, it has opened the door too wide. If some statements are analytic, what principled reason have we for denying that some of them may find (or have found) their way into theoretical centrality? The above argument does not offer such reason, for if an analytic statement were to become so central, it would not be thus revisable, no matter what sorts of epistemic difficulty may arise, and even if we adopted a new total theory. Quine may urge that theoretically central statements gain their meaning as a whole—"The unit of empirical significance is the whole of science" (p. 42). But to enter this at this point in the argument is clearly to beg the question. Quine[18] needs some account of how there can be the trivial analytic truths there are that shows why the conditions for analyticity cannot be met by statements that are of theoretical significance, and, as I say, the above modified version of the 'web of belief' argument will not of itself do the trick. Once it is granted that there are some analytic truths, it is not at all self-evident that 'revision may strike anywhere'. Pointing to interconnections in beliefs will not suffice here, for there may be *linguistic* as well as logical and empirical constraints on how we may modify our belief system. Some truths are not revisable, and, so far as I can tell, the history of science can do nothing to show that none of these are 'part of the theory', that is, potentially important. All that history has shown is that some of the truths we thought unrevisable were not. It has not shown that nothing is unrevisable, for this is not even true. And if this is so, it is hard to see how history of itself can show that nothing important is unrevisable. So, again, we need some sort of theoretical account to tell us why analyticity may be a property of some statements, but only on the condition that they play no important role for us. And

---

[18]Or, better, Quine*ans*, since Quine himself does not accept the trivial cases, not knowing what we ascribe in ascribing analyticity.

without such an account, our grounds for suspicion of analyticity cannot justify our rejecting necessities *a posteriori* for which we otherwise have good grounds.

4. Putnam on One-Criterion Terms

But there is such an account, and we need to consider it. In "The Analytic and the Synthetic," Putnam suggests that analytic truths form a special class. They share in common, he claims, that their subject terms are what he calls 'one-criterion terms' (p. 69). A one-criterion term ('T') is one that is associated with a single exceptionless 'law' of the form 'x is T if and only if x is R'. In addition, it must be the case that there are no other exceptionless laws of this form associated with the term and, further, that the right-hand side of the law is used as a (epistemic) criterion for determining whether something is (a) T.[19] With this notion of a one-criterion term, Putnam suggests that a statement is analytic just in case it states (or follows from) the exceptionless law associated with a single-criterion term. This should not be read as a definition, but it is supposed to lend some insight into what is going on in the realm of analyticity. And it seems to provide opponents of analyticity with just what they need. For if a statement holds a position in our belief system that makes it a candidate for being an important or analytic truth, then it will not in general be the case—and certainly won't be guaranteed in principle—that there will be only one (exceptionless) law (that is, the statement itself) associated with the subject of that statement. Thus, the statement will not express a one-criterion law and so, according to Putnam's account, will not be analytic.

We must ask what the 'no other laws' clause is doing in Putnam's account. Why is this a restriction upon one-criterion terms, and ultimately upon what statements can be analytic? Clearly, it is doing all the important work in explaining

[19]Putnam, "Two Dogmas Revisited," p. 89.

why there can be no significant analytic truths; it is what must be present for analyticity, but lacking for significance. So how is this constraint justified?[20]

As far as I can see, the answer is this: Suppose that we have an exceptionless truth that strikes us as plausibly analytic. If such a statement is enmeshed with our other beliefs, it is likely that we (should come to) accept other generalizations regarding the subject of that statement. Once we have a multiplicity of universal statements about a single subject, there is the possibility of conflict. The situation clearly gets worse as the number of generalizations increases, and there seems to be no ruling out the possibility that the best, or at least the simplest, way to modify our theory about this subject, at some point, will be to give up our initial generalization, the one that we thought was analytic. We shall then say that the statement was not analytic, but served to point us toward a certain subject: to (loosely) fix the reference of the subject term. So, if we accept a number of generalizations involving a subject term, (1) each of them will be subject to revision and (2) the term in question will not have an analytic definition; the various beliefs will be attempts to 'get at' a certain kind (individual, magnitude). Thus, if a term does not satisfy the 'no other laws' clause in Putnam's account, we can see why it would be unreasonable to think that the exceptionless law under consideration involving that term was analytic. It will be noted that if this exposition is right, Putnam does not need anything so strong as the 'no other exceptionless laws' clause—other laws *period*, especially if there were enough of them, would suffice to render analyticity doubtful (see "Two Dogmas Revisited," p. 58).

---

[20]Putnam could claim that he needs no justification for this clause, that it is simply what he *means* by 'one-criterion term'. But this would only shift the burden to the claim that all analytic truths are one-criterion laws. The discussion that follows can be easily understood as applying to that claim; we merely replace 'satisfies the 'no other laws' clause' (and similar expressions) with 'is a one-criterion term' (or similar expressions).

Is this a good reason for thinking that the 'no other laws' clause is a reasonable constraint upon what can count as a one-criterion term, and thus upon what statements can be analytic? We should notice that in this question, the 'thus' is superfluous. The reasons we have offered for thinking the clause reasonable *just are* reasons for thinking that theoretically central statements cannot be analytic. What is added, perhaps, is a particular specification of how it can come about, for any such central statement, that revision is warranted. But the reasons given do not really go beyond the basic Quinean considerations that we have already discussed and found wanting, and that were supposed to be explained or defended by appealing to Putnam's one-criterion-term theory of analyticity. What we have done is to appeal to Quine's arguments in defense of considerations that were supposed to make those (Quine's) very arguments more effective. The argument:

(1) Analytic truths are one-criterion laws,

(2) It is a condition on one-criterion terms that they be associated with only one (exceptionless) law,

(3) This condition will not be met by terms in theoretically central statements, and

(4) Therefore, such central statements cannot be analytic,

essentially just restates the claim that since central statements are subject to conflict, they cannot be unrevisable. If we found the argument for that latter claim to be unsatisfactory (at least for the purpose of giving us reason to reject the necessary *a posteriori*), then we shall be unimpressed with either the 'no other laws' constraint on one-criterion terms or else with the claim that analytic truths are all one-criterion laws. Either way, we are left without good theoretical reason for denying that analytic truths, given that there are some, cannot be among our important beliefs.

There is only one further way I can see to support the 'no

other laws' condition on one-criterion terms.[21] This would simply be that if we believed more than one exceptionless (biconditional) law concerning a particular subject, we would have no grounds for asserting that one rather than another stated an analytic truth. They couldn't both (all) be analytic—unless the conditions implied each other—so none must be. This is more straightforward but, I think, quite weak. It asserts, at best, that if there were more than one exceptionless law associated with a term, then we could not know that one rather than another was analytic. But even this seems to be false. We can imagine coming to know some exceptionless law about bachelors, but we would still know that the property ascribed in that law was not analytically true of bachelors and that being unmarried was. Believing an exceptionless law to hold of a subject is simply not our only criterion for judging that a statement is analytic. Thus, this defense of the 'no other laws' condition on one-criterion terms is no more successful than the more Quinean approach above and probably less so. But without such a justification, Putnam's account cannot provide us with a principled reason for thinking that there cannot be interesting analytic truths, given that there are some analytic truths. And so far as I can see, Putnam's account is the only one around that could plausibly give us such a reason. I conclude, then, that if we have good independent reason for thinking that there are necessary *a posteriori* truths, we ought to accept both them and the analytic principles to which they commit us. While the considerations of Quine and others may give us good reason to be generally skeptical about claims to analyticity, they do not give us enough reason to reject independently well-supported beliefs that commit us to analyticity.

Let me emphasize this last point to quell any suspicion that

---

[21]Or, by the same token, the claim that all analytic truths are one-criterion laws (see n. 20).

I am not giving Quine and the foes of analyticity their due. I have not argued that their arguments are bad. Indeed, I think they are quite good and do justify a general suspicion about analyticity. I think, in fact, that success in finding conceivable counterexamples to plausibly analytic statements, and lack of success in producing even parts of analytic definitions for most terms, suffices of itself to justify such suspicion. And Quine's considerations provide a theoretical background against which we can understand why there should be so little analyticity. So I am not rejecting the general suspicion. Indeed, if there are analytic general principles of individuation, so far from cutting against the general grain of such suspicion, we shall have more general grounds for believing that, in general, there are not definitions for particular names and natural kind terms. There will be but a few analytic truths, of a quite general nature, in virtue of which all (non-logical) predications of more particular terms will be both synthetic and revisable, and part of our total theory. Thus, again, I accept the general suspicion and do not think my argument warrants a free-for-all on analyticity. My argument has been for the more specific claim that we cannot use the grounds for this suspicion in order to reject independently well-confirmed claims that commit us to analyticity—even interesting analyticity. For grounds for suspicion are not grounds for firm rejection, and, as we have seen, there is nothing in anti-analyticity arguments to completely close the door on such analytic truths. We may believe that we will not find such independently well-confirmed claims, but if we do—and necessary truths *a posteriori* seem promising candidates—we must swallow both the claims and the analyticity. The justified rejection of (important) analyticity extends only so far as we do not have good independent reason to accept claims that commit us to such analyticity—and no farther.

To recap, then, I have argued that while we may have good reason for general suspicion of analyticity, we do not have strong enough grounds here to warrant the rejection of claims that commit us to analyticity and for which we have independent grounds for belief. This is because, basically, Quine does not give us good reason for the wholesale rejection of analyticity—again, most of his followers are willing to grant some analyticity. But once this is admitted, we do not have principled reason for denying that some of these analytic truths might be interesting or important. And only such grounds could warrant rejecting well-supported claims that commit us to important analyticity.

A Preliminary Conclusion

This, in effect, concludes the central argument of this book. I have argued that we both can and should preserve an empiricist account of necessity, even in the face of necessary truths *a posteriori*. We can do so by appealing to general principles of individuation that are analytic; we should do so because real necessity is unacceptable, both epistemologically and metaphysically. This left us with the worry that we had perhaps thrown out the baby with the bath water, that by showing that accepting necessary truths *a posteriori* commits us to such analyticity, what we had succeeded in doing was providing reason to reject such claims to necessity for empirical truths. But this worry, I have just argued, is unfounded. Whether or not we should believe that there are necessary truths *a posteriori* is a matter that must be decided by considering the claims themselves, in their own right, and without an eye to the consequences in terms of analyticity. If such claims can be defended successfully, then we must indeed embrace analytic principles of individuation; but we cannot deny such claims because of this consequence.

All this, however, is completely neutral on the issue of whether or not there are necessary truths *a posteriori* or analytic principles of individuation. While I shall remain effectively neutral concerning the former, I now wish to argue that, empirical necessities or no, we must have analytic principles of individuation. Nothing that has preceded depends on this. However, if it is true, then it provides additional support for the claim I have just been defending, that the analyticity to which necessities *a posteriori* commit us gives us no reason to deny these necessities—for we are committed to the analyticity anyway. Further, insofar as it is true that analytic definitions for most terms do not seem to be forthcoming, we have good reason to think that the required analyticity takes the form of general principles of individuation. It will fall out of this that there *are* necessary *a posteriori* truths, since the individuating features of particular individuals and kinds will not be analytically associated with them. Finally, if this argument is correct, it is of quite independent interest as establishing that there are important analytic truths. So, while nothing I have argued thus far depends upon the argument I am about to give, it will, if succcessful, support both my argument and the substantive claims that appear (in my major argument) only as parts of conditionals, that is, that there are necessary truths *a posteriori* and that there are analytic general principles of individuation. Throwing neutrality to the wind, then, here is why I think there must be analytic principles of individuation.

Part 2. Why There Must Be Analyticity in Individuation

I shall offer here two not wholly unrelated arguments. The first argues for the conclusion on metaphysical grounds, drawing in part on considerations adduced earlier in this book. The second argues for the conclusion on semantic grounds, claiming, basically, that such analyticity is a requirement for even approximate determinacy of reference. If the first argument is convincing, the second should be as well. However, the latter argument stands perfectly well on its own, even if the first should be found wanting.

The Metaphysical Argument

Principles of individuation, or statements of criteria of individuation, will be either analytic or synthetic. If they are synthetic, and true, this will be because they state, of the entities that are subjects of the statements, what their actual criteria of individuation are. Now, if all such statements are synthetic, it needs to be the case that the world is composed of entities that are individuated by the world—that is, that exist and have individuating features quite independently of our conventions or decisions about how to speak, or conceptually carve up the world. This is because, as I argued earlier (chapters 1 and 3), if the world is not so independently carved up, then in order for us to speak of (more or less) determinate features of the world with individuating criteria, such as individuals and kinds, *we* would have to do the carving, and the effect would be analytic principles of individuation. For it is such individuative principles that do the carving, and if these statements are not, in the first place, about how the world is (independently) segmented (for the reason that it is *not* so segmented), then they are reflections of our decisions, informed or not, concerning how to divide up the world. And such decisions are the stuff of analytic truths.[22]

It is important to keep in mind that, on the supposition that the world is not composed of independently individuated parts, our decisions are not merely to call this thing '*x*' and that kind of thing '*y*'. There are no such things to name. We decide *first* to carve the world up in a certain way by specifying individuative criteria and *then* attach the words to the 'portions-made-things' or simply to the criteria. The pic-

---

[22]For consider the decision: "Let us have some kinds individuated by their chemical structure—call them (for simplicity) 'chemical kinds'." It shall be true, as a result, that chemical kinds are individuated by their chemical structures. But this statement is made true by our decision to individuate and speak a certain way, and is thus analytic.

ture, then, is not of a set of things that we denote by a name and then endow with individuating features. As Wiggins stresses, to have the things *is to have* such features.[23] Rather, in claiming that things with such features are not in the world *per se*, we are claiming that the *things so individuated* do not, as such, belong to the world itself. The matter of these things may be so independent, but it does not have the individuating properties (as such) that makes them the things they are. This, again, is not to argue for this view; it is merely to make clear what we are committed to on the supposition that the world is not composed of independently individuated individuals and kinds. But the consequence of this picture is that we must specify individuating criteria, for example, 'unmarried man', and, as we use simpler terms to denote the now individuated items (or, if one prefers, as we state the criteria of individuation in terms of this individuative scheme), we shall wind up with analytic principles of individuation, for example, 'A bachelor is an unmarried man'. Principles of individuation would reflect our decisions rather than the independent natures of things and would thus be analytic rather than synthetic. In short, if the world is not independently carved up, in the sense of individuation, then if we are to speak of individuals and kinds as we do, there must be analytic principles of individuation.

We should note that, on this picture, it is not required that all referring terms be associated analytically with criteria of individuation. To use our earlier example, we could decide to individuate a kind according to chemical structure. This would specify, though only generally and by means of description, the individuating feature (chemical structure) of a whole class of more specific kinds. That is, for any more

---

[23]David Wiggins, *Sameness and Substance* (Cambridge: Harvard University Press, 1980), pp. 136–37, and "Ayer on Monism, Pluralism and Essence," in G. MacDonald, ed., *Perception and Identity* (Ithaca: Cornell University Press, 1979).

particular kind that is a chemical kind, it will be individuated by its chemical structure. Thus, with such general principles of individuation, we need not have analytic principles of individuation for lower-level kinds (for example, water). We may have a name for such a lower-level kind and not know, without investigation, what satisfies the individuating description set forth in the more general principle (the chemical structure). Thus, a nonindividuated world would not require that all principles of individuation be analytic, but only that some be; more particularly, what is required is that all such principles either be themselves analytic or be explained in terms of principles that are analytic, that is, have their indi-viduative character so explained.[24]

All this out of the way, I may now state the metaphysical argument. We have just been considering the claim that if the world is not independently individuated, then we must have analytic principles of individuation. My claim is that the world is not so independently individuated. Therefore, any principle of individuation is either analytic or has its indi-viduative force explained by other principles of individuation at least one of which (the final one) is analytic; there *are* analytic principles of individuation. But why should we not think that the world has parts that are individuated on their own?

My argument here will be quick though not, I hope, dirty. It draws upon two of our earlier findings. In chapter 4, I argued that there is no real necessity, that all necessity—or, at

---

[24]It is compatible with this that such an explanation may go through a number of synthetic principles; indeed, this will be the case if there are very abstract general principles governing, say, kinds of kinds of kinds. The commitment here is only that any principle of individuation be *ultimately* explained, as regards its individuative character, by some analytic princi-ple. (It will be noted that this runs parallel to our earlier noting that, for the purposes of explaining necessity, it is not required that *all* general princi-ples be analytic, only that there be enough to explain all empirical necessi-ties.)

least, all that of which we know—is grounded in analyticity. But in chapter 1, in discussing real and nominal essentialism, we saw that whether or not kinds and individuals were real or nominal entities depended upon whether or not their individuating features were so independently of our conventions. And this, in turn, depends upon whether there is real necessity. For if there is not, then necessary truths and ascriptions of necessary properties—as statements of individuation are—cannot reflect completely independent states of affairs. The truth of such statements would have to depend at least in part upon our individuative decisions, and it is from these that such statements would have their individuative and modal force. Therefore, if, as we established in chapter 4, there is no real necessity, then individuals and kinds must be but nominal existents and are not independently individuated. Individuation is an activity of ours whereby we make, rather than try to discover, divisions in the world. As a result, in accordance with our earlier considerations in this section, we must have analytic principles of individuation if we are to talk, as we do, about individuals and kinds.

That is the metaphysical argument. Short, as I said, but not, I think, without force. It has three basic premises: (1) If there is no independent individuation, then our talk about individuals and kinds must be anchored in individuating decisions and therefore analytic principles of individuation; (2) if there is independent individuation, then there must be necessary truths that are independent of our conventions, since individuative principles assert necessary connections and further are presumably themselves necessary; and (3) there is no real necessity—necessity wholly independent of our conventions. This last premise is the one most central to our concerns and thus the most thoroughly defended. The second was touched upon in our earlier discussion of Locke's nominal essentialism (pp. 18–24), but is also, I think, plausibly viewed as simply following from the very nature of individuation. And the first, though discussed but briefly here, seems fairly straightforward. Thus, as I say, I think the argument has a good deal of force. If it is correct, then we are committed to analytic principles simply by talking about individuals and kinds as we do. But while I think the argument is a good one, I realize it may not be completely convincing. There is some vagueness in the notion of 'independent individuation',[25] and some may challenge the connection between individuation and necessity. This raises questions interesting in their own right; so interesting, though, that a full discussion of them would carry us too far afield. I thus leave the argument as it stands, with whatever force it has, at least upon reflection, and hope that this is considerable.

As I say, this is in part because a discussion worthy of these issues would be too involved for our present interests. However, this sidestepping is also informed by the fact that there is another, independent argument for our commitment to analytic principles of individuation. The availability of this argument alleviates some of the need to inquire further into the premises of the metaphysical argument and allows us to leave it as it stands. The argument to which I now allude I call 'the semantic argument', as it focuses more on the semantic issue of reference than on the metaphysical issue of individuation. This makes it, I think, somewhat easier to get a hold on.

The Semantic Argument

Suppose that we do not conclude, on the basis of our findings about necessity, that there are no real, that is, independently individuated, individuals and kinds—that there are no portions of the world with criteria of identity 'built in'. We could not argue, then, that we need to make analyticity-producing individuating decisions on the grounds that there are no individuals and kinds out there waiting to be referred to. However, we would then have other grounds for our

[25]Although it seems that it is really a burden of the modal/individuative realist to make some sense of this.

claim. For there would then be *too many* entities for us to (even roughly) determinately refer to any one of them without somehow specifying their individuating criteria. Let me explain.

If we suppose that there are real, individuated entities out in the world, we must suppose that there are lots of them. In particular, there will be a good deal of entity overlap. In the case of kinds, this takes the form of coextension, or even a weaker relation of coextension in a place (or at a time) that we might call 'speech–community overlap (coextension)'. In the case of individuals, we have the sharing of matter, or, more loosely again, the sharing of matter for a significant portion of time (as with a person and his body).[26] Now, in the presence of such overlap (and I hope it is uncontroversial to suppose that we are always in its presence), how can we manage to refer to one rather than another of this multiplicity of entities?

It seems to me that there are only two possibilities here: either we do not so refer or we do so by intending, in some way, to pick out one entity rather than the others, and this in such a way as to determine analytic principles of individuation. The first possibility does not seem to amount to much, for we are perfectly capable of distinguishing among various overlapping entities and of asserting (at least by way of considering counterfactual situations) that one of each set is the object of our reference. But why, it may be asked, is the only other option that intentions determine reference? And, perhaps more pointedly, why should we think that these must be intentions that make for analyticity?

The first question is answered most straightforwardly. To put it simply, nothing else will do the trick. For when there is overlap, there is nothing actual (or, in the case of the weaker

[26]For my purposes here, it does not matter whether we think of this in terms of overlapping (distinct) individuals, or in terms of contingent identity.

relations, nothing present) in virtue of which we may refer to one rather than another of the lot. They share all actual (present, local) properties, so we cannot appeal, for instance, to causal relations between entities in the world and our use of a term. For all the relevant entities will stand in the same causal relations to those uses. If we are to even distinguish among the entities, we must focus on some feature that individuates one from the others, and if we refer to one, this must be due to our associating some term with the individuating criteria. So, consider our earlier case involving water and water$_2$ (the more superficial kind). What makes 'water' refer to water rather than water$_2$ consists (at least in part) in our intention to talk about a chemical kind, or 'the chemical structure (or deepest explanatory feature) underlying these samples'. How else could the distinction be made? But once we have seen why such intentions are required, it is just a small step to seeing why they result in analyticity.

Someone may fail to see this. "Why can we not simply use an (contingently) identifying description to fix the reference?" The answer is obvious: No merely contingent description would suffice to identify any one of the entities in question, to distinguish one entity from the others. Distinguishing them at all requires focusing on properties that one, but not the others, may (or may not) have. So if distinguishing overlapping entities is a requirement for referring to one but not all, then the fixing of reference must be a matter of using a truly individuative feature. Thus, the statement 'X's are F' in such a situation cannot be contingent. But must it be analytic? Well, as I have described the situation, the reason a term refers to what it refers to is that we have decided to use it in a certain way. In particular, it is because we have decided to use it to refer to the entity that is individuated thus: ——— ———. If all this is so, then it seems to me a straightforward matter of linguistic convention (decision) that this statement is true: 'X's are individuated by ——————' (see note 22). In sum, the phenomenon of overlapping entities requires that if our reference is to be determinate (as determinate as it is), then there must be analytic principles of individuation. We can pick them out only by their individuating features, and we can determine our words to refer to them only by deciding that a term should denote one so picked out.

As before, it is important to notice that the individuating criteria need not be specifically referred to in each case. We need not pick out water as 'the kind individuated by being H_2O'. Something more general, like 'This stuff—chemical kind' could do. In that case, it would not be analytic that water is H_2O; what would be analytic would be 'water is individuated by its chemically deep features',[27] leaving it as an empirical matter what those deep features were. Or, even more generally, what might be analytic is 'water is individuated by its *scientifically* (most) deep features',[28] leaving it empirical that water is a chemical kind rather than some other natural kind.

Now, this sort of analytic principle might be thought to be so general as to be hardly worthy of the title 'principle of individuation'. In conclusion, I wish to make two relevant remarks. First, while such intentions are quite general, they still specify—though they do not mention—what the individuating features are of the kind (or individual) referred to by the term in question. In particular, when the more specific scientific results come in, and we are able to say: 'We have discovered empirically that water is necessarily H_2O', we will be in a position to claim that the modal aspect of this truth and the explanation of our knowledge of this modality stem from our having analytically determined what are the individuating features of this stuff. Thus, though quite ab-

---

[27]Or, more precisely, 'Water is individuated by its chemically deep features if there *is* a deep chemical similarity among the samples we call 'water'; otherwise, we are talking about the (a) more superficial kind'. (This is what Putnam refers to as our 'fall-back criteria'. See "The Meaning of 'Meaning'," pp. 225, 241; also see chapter 3, pp. 58–60.)

[28]Subject to the above qualification.

stract, such analytic truths would play the role we earlier ascribed to general principles of individuation. Second, this all takes on a somewhat stronger significance if we do not grant, as we should not, that portions of the world have criteria of individuation 'built in' (p. 159). Then, while the individuative criterion 'scientifically (causally) deep features' remains quite general, we see the need for *something* if we are to have individuation at all, and we see that even something so general can suffice for this task. Individuation remains a matter of decision, whether we provide specific criteria or more general ones. It is this feature which renders the resulting criteria analytic, and the individuative (reference-determining) importance of these truths is independent of the level at which they specify their criteria.

Finally, while the metaphysical and semantic arguments each work on their own, they can also be combined to form a constructive dilemma. The world consists of independently individuated parts (individuals and kinds) or it does not. If it does not, then we need analytic principles of individuation if we are to speak of the world in terms of individuals and kinds as we do; if it does, then we need analytic principles of individuation if we are to have the kind of determinacy in reference we seem to have and think that we have. Either way, we have analytic principles of individuation, and neither way are we required to provide particular individuating criteria for each word we use. Thus, this conclusion does not clash with what we already know, that for most terms there do not seem to be analytically specified definitions, that is, necessary and sufficient conditions for the application of the term. Further, if we add this to our argument, then we may conclude, finally, that there are analytic general principles of individuation and, from this, that there are necessary truths *a posteriori*. All this is, again, inessential to our central defense of the empiricist theory of necessity. However, the arguments and conclusion of this section are certainly pertinent to our major claim (since, if they are right, the commitment to analyticity engendered by necessary truths *a posteriori* gives us no reason to reject such truths) and should at any rate give the reader something more substantive upon which to chew.

There remains one final loose end. I have, at a number of points throughout the previous chapters, suggested that our findings raise problems for causal theories of reference. Earlier in this chapter, I claimed more particularly that the causal theory of reference cannot be cited as a reason to reject analyticity, since its very plausibility requires that it be able to accommodate analytic principles. My aim in the next and final chapter is to bear out these claims and to show how the defense of empiricist metaphysics that has been here presented provides also a defense of basic empiricist semantics.

6 *Analyticity and Reference*

My CENTRAL AIM in this book has been to defend the basic empiricist view about necessity against the challenge raised by the alleged discoveries of necessary truths that are synthetic and *a posteriori*. I hope that the previous chapters have accomplished this. But the challenge of real essentialism is only part of a (at least) two-pronged assault upon empiricism. While these empirical necessities threaten empiricist metaphysics, the causal theory of reference is supposed to be cutting away the legs of empiricist semantics; the full effect is thought to be an empiricist swan song and the emergence of a comprehensive realist worldview.

Having defended empiricism about modality, I should like in this final chapter to turn to a defense of empiricist semantics. No doubt, there are other facets to the realist/empiricist debate, and as I make no attempt to address them all, I make no comprehensive claims about the adequacy of empiricism against the full-scale realist challenge. However, I have made throughout this book a number of claims about the theory of reference, and, in particular, about what I take to be the consequences for reference of our account of necessity. There are two related reasons for my having made such claims and for my confronting the semantic challenge here. The first is that the causal theory of reference and real essentialism are more or less explicit compatriots. As I have noted, the presentation and defense of necessary truths *a posteriori* first arose in discussions of the causal theory of reference; they provide a united front.[1] So there is some call for saying something about the causal theory in an extended discussion of the necessary *a posteriori*. The second and far more important reason is that I believe that there is a fairly deep connection between theories of reference and views on modality. In particular, I think the empiricist view of necessity requires the basic position of empiricist semantics, and that the causal theory of reference presupposes essentialism[2] and so will have the consequence that there are necessary truths *a posteriori*. And even if this strong claim about the causal theory is false, it remains true that the causal theory allows for such necessary truths, and that this is a fundamental motivation for the theory. So it is no accident that the necessary *a posteriori* has been presented within discussions of the causal theory; similarly, it should be no surprise that I think my defense of empiricism about necessity has consequences for the theory of reference. Thus, I conclude this treatise on necessity with a discussion of what I take to be its implications for the theory of reference both generally and more particularly for empiricist and causal theories of reference.

In this chapter, I focus my remarks around two basic claims: first, that the basic claim of empiricist semantics is true, and, second, that the causal theory of reference is either false or compatible with this basic claim. This second may seem hardly to be a distinct claim at all—it follows from and seems to add nothing to the first. However, there is a reason

---

[1]Kripke, *Naming and Necessity*; Putnam, "The Meaning of 'Meaning'."

[2]'Presupposes' is here used in its ordinary, nonphilosophical sense: if p presupposes q, then for p to be true, q must be true (this is probably not sufficent for presupposition; what is needed in addition is probably some sort of relevance condition). I do *not* intend the more technical sense, in which if p presupposes q, then q must be true for p to have a truth value at all.

for the separate presentation of this second claim. For as I have already suggested, I believe that there is a reason beyond the truth of empiricist semantics that makes it the case that the causal theory of reference, if it is to be true as well, must be compatible with empiricist semantics. There are features internal to the causal theory that, when combined with my findings about necessity, require that the causal theory acknowledge analytic principles of individuation that suffice for empiricist semantics. Thus, even if one has not accepted empiricist semantics (if, for instance, one is not committed to any semantic theory), one should still think that the causal theory of reference must be compatible with empiricist semantics if it is to be true. For this reason, it is worth a discussion of this requirement of the causal theory beyond my argument for the truth of basic empiricist semantics.

In addition, the very idea that the causal theory could be compatible with empiricism may strike many as unintelligible or preposterous—they are rival accounts of reference. Thus, it might be thought that if empiricist semantics could be vindicated, by that token the causal theory would be falsified; to say that if empiricist semantics is true, the causal theory must be either false or compatible with it, is to add a trivially true but practically meaningless disjunct. However, if it is true that, given my account of necessity, forces internal to the causal theory require its compatibility with empiricist semantics, then the possibility of their being compatible should not be dismissed out of hand. To so dismiss this possibility is not quite to accuse the causal theory of internal incoherence (since my account of necessity is not part of the causal theory), but it would be quite close. It is thus worth seeing how we might reconcile the theories, and this is part of what we shall discuss consequent to my argument that the causal theory, if true, must be compatible with empiricist semantics. If such a compromise cannot be worked out, so much the worse for the causal theory, both internally and because of the truth of empiricist semantics. If, however, one can consistently maintain both views, then the causal theory of reference is not the radical theory many of its proponents have taken it to be, and it is no weapon that can be used against empiricism. As with the necessary *a posteriori*, the causal theory, by requiring empiricism, can do nothing to overthrow empiricism, but provides, at best, an interesting extension of that view.

Finally, aside from arguing for doctrinal points, that is, that the basic empiricist semantic view is true and that the causal theory of reference is either false or compatible with empiricism, I wish to provide a broad positive picture of reference that results from our metaphysical inquiry, in particular if we accept that there are necessary truths *a posteriori* and deny that most terms have analytic definitions. We may then ask how this picture fits in with the claims of empiricists or causal theorists. As might be expected, while I think there might be some issue over whether this account of reference is in accord with causal theories, there should be no issue over whether it is a theory in the empiricist tradition.

Empiricist Semantics

What is the basic claim of empiricist semantics? Or, put another way, what makes a semantic theory empiricist?

As it is often understood, empiricist semantic theory rests on the claim that words achieve their reference through ideas or definitions analytically associated with the words, the referents of these words being those things that satisfy these definitions.[3] I have claimed earlier that this is not essential to

---

[3]Or, at least, this is the theory for names and kind terms. This cannot, of course, be the *whole* semantic story, for we need to know how the ideas or definitions achieve *their* reference. But our concern here is with names and kind terms, insofar as we are concerned with relating empiricist semantics to the causal theory of reference, and the causal theory is concerned principally with these sorts of referring expressions.

the empiricist account. Just as the view that all necessary truths are analytic is a particular theory within the more general view that all necessity is rooted in our conventions, so this theory of reference falls within a more general and fundamental semantic position, namely, that there must be conventional individuative features in language (at least, in a language that talks about individuated things).

Aside from the analogy, the claim that this more general semantic view is what characterizes the empiricist position is supported by the fact that this is the view that goes with their position on necessity. That is, if empiricists can countenance more complex conventions in virtue of which necessary *a posteriori* truth can be explained, then they need not be committed to such particular conventional elements as definitions in their semantic theory. Unless the unified empiricist picture is incoherent, it cannot be the case that empiricist metaphysics can countenance what empiricist semantics forbids. Further, I suggested earlier that empiricist semantics is informed by its metaphysics. A central motivation for thinking that we need conventional individuating features is the belief that the world is not composed of independently sorted things and types. If this is so, then while it may be natural to think that the sorting we provide comes in the form of particular definitions, there is nothing here to mandate that this is how the demand for individuation be incorporated into our language. If more complex conventions can do the job, there is nothing in the reasoning that supports empiricist semantics to rule this out. Thus, again, while empiricists have tended to think that each name and kind term has an analytic definition, their fundamental view is that we must have conventional individuating elements in our language. Put another way, a good empiricist can tolerate revision in the 'analytic definitions' theory of reference so long as such revision preserves some conventional feature that provides, abstractly or more particularly, the boundary conditions for the reference of our terms.

Perhaps the simplest way to see this, if it is not already clear from the above considerations, is to suppose that what I have called 'general principles of individuation' are analytic, reference-determining conventions. Chemical compound terms, say, would refer (rigidly) to whatever microstructure was common to and most deeply explanatory of (enough of) the samples that we call by those names; 'water', thus, refers to H_2O. Now, if this were the case, we would not have analytic definitions characteristic of traditional empiricist semantic theories. But I think it intuitively clear that an account proposing such a mechanism of reference would fall squarely within the empiricist tradition. We still have, for kind terms, what is basically 'reference by description'. While there is not a description for every term, every term (or every individual or kind term) is a term of some kind, and the rules of reference for the term-types are given by conventional descriptions. So again, and finally, if such a theory counts as empiricist, then it is not essential to empiricist semantic theory that all terms have analytic definitions. And the judgment that such a theory *is* empiricist is supported, I think, both intuitively (that is, by fairly straightforward similarity judgments) and theoretically (in accordance with the reasons preceding this paragraph).

Now that we have some clearer idea of what the fundamental empiricist semantic claim is, how is it supported by our findings regarding necessity?

Vindicating Empiricist Semantics

Much of what is relevant here has already been discussed. If there is no real necessity, then there are no real (as opposed to nominal) essences. There is thus no real individuation and so there are no real subjects of individuation as such—that is, there are no real (again, as opposed to nominal) individuals or kinds. If all that is right, then if there is no real necessity, then the reference of our names and kind terms must be determined, in part, by conventionally set boundaries. This is to say that if there is no real necessity, and we have seen that there is not, then the fundamental claim of empiricist semantics is true.

Similarly, if there is no real necessity, then we cannot, simply by ostension or a series of applications of a term, establish reference to modally extended entities. Insofar as our means of determining reference makes it come out that we can make true, nontrivial essential predications, there must be something conventional in these means that makes this so. Some sort of intension, of the sort that makes for analytic truths, must regulate our modal assertions. For if there is no real necessity, there is nothing in the external world that can determine the truth or falsity of such assertions. One can, of course, deny that there are any such true essential predications. But for one thing, this is coming to look increasingly implausible, and, for another, it is primarily by appeal to such predications that empiricism has been cast into doubt.

Most briefly, the connection between the metaphysical arguments I have presented and basic empiricist semantics is this. It seems to be part and parcel of our use of certain kinds of terms (names and kind terms, for instance) that we can use them to make counterfactual assertions, some true and some false, about how things could have been. But, according to our earlier considerations, there is nothing in the (mind-independent) world in virtue of which such assertions could have a truth value. It must be, then, that this role is filled by conventions of ours that determine modal extension and, thus, that the basic empiricist semantic claim is true. There must be, at some level, analytic principles of individuation.

Now, so far as I can tell, none of this cuts directly against a causal theory of reference. The considerations do not specify anything very particular about how reference is determined—they only show that somewhere in the story, conventional individuating decisions need to be made. Thus, the only direct implication for causal theories of reference is that they must be able to accommodate these conventions, that is, to accord them a role, if they are to be adequate. This is not, of course, an insignificant finding. It shows that insofar as a causal theory can provide a satisfactory account of reference, it must be compatible with basic empiricist semantics. If one wishes to urge the radical nature of his causal theory, its dramatic break with more traditional accounts and its replacement (contrast: modification) of empiricist semantics, then one ensures the falsity of his theory. But, again, while some causal theorists seem to have this view about the historical place of their theory, it is not clear that they need to claim that their theory is incompatible with empiricism.[4] Indeed, I shall now argue that they should not—not merely because empiricism is true, but because features internal to the theory strongly indicate the need for compatibility with empiricism. If this is so, then we have another argument to the effect that the causal theory must be compatible with empiricism if it is to be true. But, in addition, we will have even stronger reason for thinking that a reasonable causal theorist need not insist on this incompatibility of his with earlier theories. For that would not only ensure the falsity of his view given the facts, but it would come quite close to ensuring the falsity of his view *come what may*. All this strongly suggests that there must be a way of understanding the causal theory so that an advocate need not renounce basic empiricist semantics; we will close this chapter with a suggestion about how one can be both a causal theorist and an empiricist.

The argument that the causal theory requires the truth of basic empiricist semantics has two parts. The first and major part is an argument for the claim that the causal theory pre-

---

[4]Note that they will not typically put the point this way. Rather, it is claimed that, since their theory is true, traditional theories are false. But this, of course, requires that the theories be incompatible.

supposes essentialism. The second part is merely a restatement of what we have already seen, that the only essentialism we can accept is nominal essentialism, which requires that there be analytic principles of individuation and thus that basic empiricist semantics be true. What we need to see, then, is the argument for the first premise, that the causal theory of reference presupposes essentialism.[5]

Essentialism and the Causal Theory

Nathan Salmon has recently argued that one cannot derive essentialism from the causal theory of reference and thus that one can accept the causal theory of reference while renouncing essentialism.[6] I am in a good deal of sympathy with the

[5]While my argument will differ in some details, and in the use to which I wish to put it, it will resemble an argument of Paul Coppock's in his fine review of *Reference and Essence*. Our arguments were reached independently.

[6]Salmon is explicit about believing that not only can no particular essentialist conclusions be derived from the causal theory, but also "It would seem that acceptance of the theory of direct reference *per se* presents no obstacle whatsoever to the anti-essentialist position" (Salmon 1981, p. 216; see also p. 264). While I shall be accepting the first of these claims, whether or not my discussion cuts against the second claim depends on whether the sort of essentialism I shall argue is required by the causal theory needs to be anything more than what Salmon calls 'trivial essentialism' (p. 83, n. 3). My guess is that it must be, since for the essentialism to be trivial, the essential predications must be trivial, and this can only be if the predications are either (1) logically true of all subjects or (2) otherwise analytic. But predicates of type (1) will not serve the individuating purpose I argue is required for the causal theory to get going, and if we have predicates of type (2) serving this purpose, then it would seem that the causal theory would fall to a more old-fashioned empiricist theory of reference. However, it might be important, for Salmon's purposes, to distinguish between a nontrivial essentialist commitment and a commitment to nontrivial essentialism: the former would be present only when a principle (theory) itself entailed (perhaps with the help of modally uninteresting premises) some particular statement of the form $\ulcorner(\exists x) \,\square\, [\text{Exists } x \supset \phi\,(x)]\urcorner$, where

spirit of Salmon's major claim. I agree with him that there are not general mechanisms for cranking out necessary *a posteriori* truths by appending unproblematic empirical facts to the causal theory. I agree that one can accept the causal theory and deny that water is necessarily H_2O. I deny, however, that one can accept the causal theory and reject essentialism altogether (see note 6 on whether this represents a conflict with Salmon's position). The causal theory, in my view, presupposes essentialism and so entails it. This is not to say that it presupposes, or entails, any *particular* essentialist claims—here again, I agree with Salmon. However, I believe that there must be *some* such essentialist truths if the causal theory is true. The commitment to essentialism I find in the causal theory is found in the theory itself—it does not result from combining the causal theory with empirical facts. Thus, while I agree with Salmon that essentialism cannot be derived from the causal theory by deriving instances of essential predications, I think it can be 'derived' in another way, namely by showing that the truth of essentialism is required for the truth of the causal theory. And, further, I believe that Salmon's own arguments can be used to establish this. That is, if Salmon is correct about the covert essentialism of certain sorts of statements—on which grounds he rejects the deriva-

---

this statement is not itself trivially true, while the latter would be encumbered more easily, by merely requiring *that there be* some truths of that form. Here, I would agree with Salmon that the causal theory does not involve a nontrivial essentialist commitment; however, for the truth of his claim stated at the start of this note (see also Salmon 1981, p. 264), it would seem that the stronger claim, that the causal theory does not have a commitment to nontrivial essentialism, must also be true, and it is this claim I shall be denying. At any rate, if I understand Salmon correctly, it is the first claim, with which I agree, that is of particular importance to him. And as will also become clear, I agree also with his claim that "the theory of direct reference can no more *solve* the difficult problem of essentialism than it can solve the mind-body problem" (p. 218). See also his "How *Not* to Derive Essentialism from the Theory of Reference," *Journal of Philosophy* 76 (1979): 703–25.

tion of essentialism—then essentialism is smuggled into what Putnam has called 'the empirical presupposition' of the causal theory of reference.[7] But from this it follows that if the causal theory of reference is true, so then is essentialism. To see this, we must first get the lay of the land.

Salmon's Reconstruction

The key element in the causal theory of reference is that words get their referents in virtue of causal relations holding between uses of the words and (typically) extralinguistic objects. This breaks with older theories, according to which the reference of a term is determined by its sense or definition. Ordinary names were thought to be disguised definite descriptions,[8] and general terms were thought to have analytic definitions that specified the criteria for belonging to the kind named by the term. But according to the causal theory, words hook into their referents without these intermediaries. It is for this reason that Salmon calls the new theory 'the theory of *direct* reference'.[9]

Now, as we have mentioned, Salmon is concerned with the attempt to derive essentialism from this theory, with the

---

[7]Putnam, "The Meaning of 'Meaning'," p. 225. See below, pp. 184–90.

[8]One need not think, as Russell did, that names are not really names, but rather disguised descriptions, in order to think that the referents of ordinary names are determined by their senses. I put it this way here only for its familiarity. See Russell, "Knowledge by Acquaintance and Knowledge by Description," in *Mysticism and Logic* (London: Longmans, Green, 1911), and "The Philosophy of Logical Atomism," in *Logic and Knowledge*, ed. R. C. Marsh (London: George Allen and Unwin, 1956). For the non-Russellian formulation, see Frege, "On Sense and Reference," in *Translations from the Philosophical Writings of Gottlob Frege*, ed. P. T. Geach and M. Black (Totowa, N.J.: Rowman and Littlefield, 1980), and Carnap, *Meaning and Necessity*.

[9]Salmon, *Reference and Essence*, pt. 1.

help only of premises that are themselves modally neutral. After carefully laying out the structure of the referential mechanism, according to the causal theory, and considering the sorts of empirical necessities that have been proposed by advocates of the causal theory, Salmon constructs the following general argument form, which he claims to be the mechanism through which essentialism is supposed to be derived.[10] More accurately, he presents two mechanisms of the same general form that are supposed to churn out particular *a posteriori* necessary truths; one mechanism (the I-mechanism) is for essential truths about individuals, while the other (the K-mechanism) is for essential truths about kinds. And since essentialism is the claim that there are such truths, the mechanisms presented are those through which essentialism is to be derived. Here, straight from Salmon, are the argument forms:

    (1) It is necessarily the case that: something is a (bit of) v if and only if it is an instance of *dthat*[11] (the K-kind that has the property of being ϕ).

    (2) Some instance of the K-kind that has the property of being ϕ has the Ψ-property of being ψ.

    (3) Being an instance of the same K-kind as something con-

---

[10]One will notice some resemblance with the sort of derivation I presented in chapter 2, *roughly* with my general principles corresponding to Salmon's third premise (see below), and the rest of the correspondence being somewhat messier. The difference reflects our concerns—Salmon wishes to carve out carefully the input of the theory of reference, while I wish to carve out the empirical input. The similarity results from our seeing the same structure in the situation; while Salmon's book came out before I started work on this one, I had formed my view on this matter before becoming aware of Salmon's work.

[11]*Dthat* is Kaplan's indexical operator; it operates on a given singular term, ϕ, and makes it into a rigid designator of whatever ϕ designates in the original context. See Kaplan, "Dthat" and "On the Logic of Demonstratives," in P. French, T. Uehling, and H. Wettstein, eds., *Contemporary Perspectives in the Philosophy of Language* (Minneapolis: University of Minnesota Press, 1979a).

sists, at least in part, in having the same Ψ-property that the given thing has.

(4) Therefore, it is necessarily the case that: every (bit of) v is ψ.

(Where v is a common noun, K-kind is a generic kind predicate that subsumes v, Ψ is a 'hidden structural property',[12] and ψ expresses the property of being a hidden structural property of a certain specified sort.)[13]

This will be much easier to understand if we take an instance—let us derive an essential property of cats:

(1′) It is necessarily the case that: something is a cat if and only if it is an instance of *dthat* (the same species of which Morris is a member).

(2′) Morris is a mammal.

(3′) Being a member of the same species as something consists, at least in part, in being a member of the same biological class.

(4′) Therefore, it is necessarily the case that: all cats are mammals.[14]

Put plainly, (1) represents the mechanism of reference as proposed by the direct theory. It is the way in which one introduces a term as a rigid designator. (2) attributes some property to (an instance of) the class referred to as specified in (1), and (3) claims that the property attributed in (2) is of the sort that determines what it is to be a member of the same general kind (here, biological species) to which the kind in question (here, cats) belongs. Of course, in presenting one's

[12]It is inessential for the Ψ-property (and, so, for ψ) to be a 'hidden structural property', although this is a fair supposition. All we really need here is for Ψ to be a property of being a certain property and for ψ to be an instance of that kind of property (see Salmon, *Reference and Essence*, p. 170, bottom).

[13]Ibid., pp. 168, 170.

[14]Compare ibid., p. 167.

proposals, one does not randomly pick out properties. What one uses in premise (2) will depend on what one uses in premise (3), that is, on the sort of property in which one takes sameness of this (kind of) kind to consist.

The I-mechanism, whereby one derives essential properties of individuals, looks similar and has the same underlying structure:

(5) It is necessarily the case that: $\alpha = dthat\ (\beta)$.

(6) β has the Ψ-property of being ψ.

(7) Being the very same individual (of kind I) as something consists, at least in part, in having the same Ψ-property.

(8) Therefore, it is necessarily the case that: α, if it exists, is ψ.[15]

To see an instance, substitute 'Margaret Truman' for α, 'that person' for β, 'origin' for Ψ, and 'the daughter of Bess Truman' for ψ.

Again, the first premise results from the theory of reference, the second represents an ordinary empirical fact, and the third claims that the property attributed in the second premise is of a kind that determines what it is to be the same individual (of a certain kind).

However complicated this looks, the basic pattern should be easy enough to understand. And once you have gotten it, there is no problem in seeing how to derive necessary truths that are *a posteriori* (since the second premise ((2) or (6)) must be gained from experience) and, *ipso facto*, essentialism.

In seeing how the derivations are supposed to be done, one should also see why they must be done in this way, that is, why premises of the sort Salmon describes are needed to get from the theory of reference to the essentialist conclusions. Premise forms (2) and (6) should be obvious enough—one

[15]Ibid., p. 173.

cannot conclude that x is necessarily a unless one uses the premise that x *is* a (unless, of course, the former is a conceptual truth—but, then, unless 'a' is a logical predicate true of all things, 'x' will not have gotten its reference as described by the causal theory; 'x is a' will be, in that case, analytic). But if one is to get the essentialist conclusions, there must be, in addition, a premise regarding the sort of property that is mentioned in the empirical premise. For, obviously, not all properties of an individual (members of kinds) are necessary (*pace* certain interpretations of Spinoza and Leibniz). Of course, the additional premise need not say that being a K (or an I) consists in ψ, where ψ is the property mentioned in (2) or (6)—indeed, with such a premise, the empirical premise would be unnecessary. Rather, the premise needs to say something more general, like 'Belonging to the kind of which K is an instance (Being the same individual as I) consists, in part, in Ψ, where Ψ is the sort of property mentioned in (2) ((6)). The key features here are (i) saying what sameness (for the kind of kind or individual) consists in and (ii) the properties expressed in the second premise being of the sort in which this sameness resides.

Another way of putting the point is to say that the derivation is subject to two constraints: a 'sameness' constraint and an empirical constraint. The latter is needed to state what feature the individual or kind actually has, while the former is needed to state what being the same consists in for the individual or kind in question; these constraints are reflected in premises (2) and (3) ((6) and (7)). It should by now be clear, I hope, that unless one meets these two constraints, that is, has premises of the sort Salmon describes, it will be quite impossible to derive necessities that are *a posteriori*. One might say that the empirical premise is needed for the *a posteriority*, while the sameness premise is needed for the necessity. So I think it is safe to say that Salmon is giving the 'essence from reference' derivers a fair run for their money.

Salmon's Argument

We are now ready to see how Salmon responds to the proposed derivations, or, more properly, to the derivation forms. Clearly, the first two premises in each case are unproblematic. The first come from the direct theory of reference, while the second are simple empirical claims, asserting ordinary attributes of individuals (members of kinds). Any objection, then, must arise from the third premises, or what I have called the 'sameness' premises. And, no surprise, here is where Salmon finds his target. Any premises satisfying forms (3) or (7) that are strong enough to entail the desired conclusions will be essentialist principles—they could generate the desired conclusions without the help of the theory of reference. As Salmon puts it, they have 'nontrivial essentialist import'.[16] Rather than being modally innocuous empirical claims, these statements assert necessary conditions for membership in a certain (kind of) kind, or for being a given individual (of a certain kind). These are metaphysical positions with modal commitments, and by making them, Salmon rightly claims, the 'essentialism-deriver' begs the question, hence failing in his project.

This should hardly be surprising. As ordinarily understood, statements of the form 'to be (an) *F* is to be (a) *G*' are statements about the essence—the 'what it is to be'—of *F*. Indeed, when we ask about the essence of a thing, we ask, 'What is it to be (an) *F*?' and the answer will generally be of the above form. But statements of forms (3) and (7) are just

---

[16]Ibid., p. 184. Salmon takes a principle to have essentialist import if, supplemented by modally trivial premises, one can derive consequences of the form ⌜($\exists x$) $\Box$ [Exists (x) $\supset$ ϕ (x)]⌝. Such principles have *nontrivial* essentialist import if these consequences are not themselves trivially true. See *Reference and Essence*, p. 83, n.3. See also Terence Parsons, "Essentialism and Quantified Modal Logic," *The Philosophical Review* 78 (1969): 35–52.

such statements, only at a one-step remove.[17] Rather than giving the essence of some kind directly, they give the essence for the kind of kind—they specify which type of features of the (particular) kind are to be taken as defining membership in that kind. Such statements differ from ordinary essential predications only in virtue of specifying the essential features more generally, for example, by 'chemical structure' rather than 'H_2O', so as to leave it for empirical inquiry to fill in the (more specific) blank. The important point here, to restate, is that insofar as the particular statements are essentialist statements, so are their more general counterparts. Once Salmon shows that such statements are required for the derivation of essentialism, the party is over. It is but an afterthought to point out that such statements embody essentialism themselves.

So much for exposition—or simple restatement—of Salmon's position on these matters. It is not my purpose here to consider whether anyone has really thought otherwise. Even philosophers who take (at least some) principles of forms (3) and (7) to be *a posteriori* results of science[18] would, or at least should, see the modal assertions inherent in such claims and, thus, their metaphysical character. This being so, the project is perhaps best seen not as that of attempting to derive essentialism from the theory of reference, but rather, as that of clearing the way for, or accommodating, (real) essentialism by allowing us to use the world to define the boundaries of kinds rather than stipulating analytic definitions for the task.[19]

[17]The reader will notice that the relationship here is the same as that between particular analytic definitions and analytic general principles of individuation.

[18]Keith Donnellan appears to be one such philosopher; see his "Rigid Designators, Natural Kinds and Individuals." However, he may have shifted away from this view, at least as regards kinds; see "Kripke and Putnam on Natural Kind Terms," in C. Ginet and S. Shoemaker, eds., *Knowledge and Mind* (New York: Oxford University Press, 1983).

[19]See, however, Salmon's motivation for attributing the 'derivation the-

But what I now wish to claim is that if Salmon's criticism is correct—and I believe that it is—then it cannot be the case both that the causal theory of reference is true and that essentialism is false; one cannot responsibly accept the causal theory while renouncing essentialism.[20] The causal theory, as I have said, presupposes essentialism. For let us characterize Salmon's 'anti-derivation' argument as follows: (1) The derivations require premises of forms (3) or (7) (Let us call these '*S*-sentences'—'*S*' for 'sameness'), and (2) Such premises are (express, smuggle in, embody, entail) nontrivial essentialist positions. What I shall argue in the following section is that the causal theory of reference presupposes that there are true *S*-sentences.[21] I do not think this needs to be very vigorously argued, nor should it be surprising—it is, indeed, freely admitted by proponents of the causal theory. But if Salmon is correct that *S*-sentences have nontrivial essentialist import, then it will follow that the causal theory can be true only if essentialism is true. And, as we have seen, this means that the truth of the causal theory requires the truth of basic empiricist semantics—for the only acceptable essentialism is nominal essentialism, and this rests upon conventional principles of individuation.

The 'Empirical Presupposition' of the Causal Theory of Reference

Perhaps it is best to let Putnam, as a founding father of the causal theory, make what I consider to be the crucial point:

---

sis' to some philosophers (*Reference and Essence*, pp. 91–92, n. 11 and 98–99). Whatever the standing here, Salmon's project is certainly an interesting and well-motivated one.

[20]Contrast Salmon, *Reference and Essence*, p. 216, 264. But see n. 6, this chapter.

[21]Compare Coppock, p. 266.

Suppose I point to a glass of water and say, 'This liquid is called water.'. . . . My 'ostensive definition' of water has the following empirical presupposition: that the body of liquid I am pointing to bears a sameness relation (say, x *is the same liquid as y*, or x *is the same$_L$ as y*) to most of the stuff I and other speakers in my linguistic community have on other occasions called 'water'. . . . The key point is that the relation same$_L$ is a *theoretical* relation: whether something is or is not the same liquid as *this* may take an indeterminate amount of scientific investigation to determine.[22]

By calling this an 'empirical presupposition', I take it that Putnam means that in order for the sort of 'baptisms', ostensive introductions, or, more generally, demonstrative reference fixings to occur *and to take* in the way proposed by causal theorists, it must be the case that the world is a certain way. If there are not sameness relations holding among portions of the world, then I cannot point to this thing and determine an extension for the word I introduce (beyond, perhaps, this particular).[23] In addition, Putnam is concerned with another point in his use of 'empirical'—he wants to maintain that just what the sameness relations (for example, for this liquid) consist in are empirical matters.[24] This is quite important when one contrasts the direct theory with more traditional theories to which it is presented as a rival. For on the old view, (general) words have analytic definitions that specify

[22]Putnam, "The Meaning of 'Meaning'," p. 225.

[23]Although I would deny even this; see, for instance, chapter 3, pp. 52–56.

[24] Putnam seems to want to maintain that the issues are empirical all the way up, i.e., what sameness consists in for *kinds* of kinds (liquids/chemical compounds), etc. Or, at least, so his earlier self seems to want to maintain. Putnam now seems to believe, along with the view I have been urging, that at some level or other, what counts as the same must be determined by convention—and further (though this seems hard to believe) that he has *always* maintained this. See his "Why There Isn't a Ready-Made World," in *Realism and Reason.*

the respects in which things must be similar if they are both to belong to the kind named by the word. But on the new view, there are no (analytic) definitions. The respects in which things must be similar to belong to the named kind are determined *by the world*, and just what features these are is determined by empirical inquiry. There is no *a priori* way to know that being water consists in being (composed of) H_2O, nor, even less, that being the same liquid as *this* (pointing to water) consists in such composition.

Now, let us consider Putnam's claim that his ostensive definition presupposes that the body of liquid to which he is pointing bears the same$_L$ relation to other stuff in the world. The reason for this is simple—it is the point of the causal theory that our kind terms get their reference not through (analytic) definitions, but through our use of them as standing for certain kinds. Rather than having conventions like " 'Water' means 'the clear, freezable liquid that covers four-fifths of the Earth's surface'," whereby our words get their reference, we apply words to various particulars (sometimes there will be a baptismal ceremony, but nothing in the theory (or this discussion) requires this) and intend our words to denote the kind of thing of which these are instances. And, obviously, for our words to denote kinds, there have to *be* kinds.

> We use 'gold' as a term for a certain *kind* of thing.[25]
> The original concept of cat is: *that kind of thing.*[26]

It is worth expanding just a bit more upon why this is required by the causal theory. As we have noted, the heart of the theory is the claim that (in general) words get their referents directly, rather than through other words or ideas. Other words are used at best to fix reference, not to give defini-

---

[25]Kripke, *Naming and Necessity*, p. 118.
[26]Ibid., p. 122.

tions. But what is directly referred to? Onto what is the word attached? In the case of singular names, the word grabs onto an individual, while in the case of general terms, it grabs onto a kind, a magnitude, or what have you. If no individual or kind is *there*, there is nothing for the word to latch onto.[27] To restate a point made earlier, whereas empiricists have called upon definitions to specify the respects in which something must resemble other things called '*F*' in order to be (an) *F*, causal theorists call upon the world to determine the relevant respects. If the world is not up to this task, then reference cannot work in the way proposed by the causal theory. So there is a presupposition about the world that must be true if the causal theory can be a true account of reference. Vaguely put, it is the supposition that the world is divided up into individuals and kinds; one can see this supposition made in premises (1) and (5) of Salmon's reconstructions. These are the premises, you will recall, that come straight from the theory of reference.

We turn, then, to the question that has obviously been lingering in the background of this entire discussion: Is the presupposition that the world is divided up into individuals and kinds free of nontrivial essentialist import?[28] Can one accept this supposition while rejecting essentialism?

It will come as no surprise that I think the answer to these questions is no. Perhaps more surprising is my belief that a good part of the reason is to be found in Salmon's uncovering of the essentialist character of *S*-sentences. For the claim that the world is divided up into individuals and kinds *just is* the claim that there are sameness relations that hold between things and in virtue of which they belong to the same kind

[27]And if there are many individuals or kinds, we are threatened with radical indeterminacy, but this is a separate point; see chap. 5, 'The Semantic Argument'.

[28]See n. 6 for a distinction between nontrivial essentialist commitment and a commitment to nontrivial essentialism. In asking about essentialist import, I am asking about the latter.

(or are the same individual). The existence of individuals and kinds requires identity conditions for these individuals and kinds, and, as Salmon argues, these will not be free of essentialist import.[29] For again, statements of identity conditions will have the form of S-sentences: they assert that in which sameness consists.

Let me try to make the point in another way. Suppose that there are no true S-statements, that is, suppose statements of the form: 'Being an instance of the same kind (Being the same individual) as something consists, at least in part, in having the same Ψ-property[30] that the given thing has' all to be false. In such a case, there will be nothing in which the identity of (any) individuals or membership in (any) kinds consists. But is this not just to suppose that there are no individuals and kinds in the world? As I have argued earlier, it is just these boundaries that make the world into a realm of articulate, individuated entities rather than a lump of stuff—the metaphysical counterpart of William James's "buzzin' bloomin' confusion." If this is so, then to suppose that there are no true S-sentences is to suppose that there is no way for words to get their referents as described by the causal theory; contrapositively, if reference is as depicted by the causal theory, then there must be true S-statements, and consequently, essentialism must also be true.

There is another feature of the causal theory that perhaps allows one to more easily see the modal requirements the theory carries with it. This is that terms get introduced as *rigid designators*: they denote whatever they do in all possible

---

[29]Must the essentialistic import be nontrivial? Not for there to be individuals and kinds *per se*. However, if all of the essentialist consequences of the true S-sentences are trivial, then presumably the negative thrust of the causal theory will be mistaken, as we would have rampant, defining-style analyticity. See n. 6.

[30]In the limiting case, the essential property will itself be named (e.g., being an unmarried man).

worlds.[31] But this brings out clearly that we are going to need sameness relations that hold not only in the actual world, but that determine the relevant sameness in all possible worlds. The presupposition that there is a relation of sameness is the supposition of a *transworld* relation: it is the requirement that there be a relation, say, same$_L$, that can hold between occupants of different possible worlds.[32] But, as Salmon points out, such a sameness relation will not be without essentialist import. Transworld sameness (identity) conditions must involve modal assertions, or at least have modal implications, and the truth of such assertions entails essentialism.

Let me reemphasize that the causal theory does not, according to this argument, require one to be an essentialist of the sort who believes that water is necessarily H_2O. Just which S-sentences are true and, hence, which particular necessities there are, is left undetermined by the truth of the causal theory. One cannot simply plug particular empirical findings into the causal theory and crank out particular essentialist truths; one cannot derive essentialism from the causal theory in the manner Salmon discusses. However, this does not show that essentialism is not entailed more directly—*not* through instances of true essential predications, but through the nature of the theory itself and the general demands it makes upon the world. If my argument is correct, then *some* S-sentences must be true if the causal theory is; one cannot both accept the causal theory and reject essentialism. Again, to emphasize once more my central point in establishing this

---

[31]This is not to say that it is necessarily true that 'water' refers to water, but rather that, when discussing counterfactual situations using English, 'water' refers always to *this stuff* and never, say, to grape juice—even if the natives call grape juice 'water', use it to wash their clothes, etc. See premise-forms (1) and (5) for the commitment here. See again Coppock, review of *Reference and Essence*, p. 266.

[32]This is understood and pointed out by Putnam, pp. 231–32.

conclusion, since the truth of essentialism requires the truth of nominal essentialism, and hence that there be conventional individuating principles, and since the basic empiricist semantic claim is that there *are* such principles, it follows that if the causal theory is true, then so is the basic empiricist semantic claim. Causal theorists must give up their claim either to radical overthrow or to truth: they cannot have it both ways.

A Weaker Argument

There will, I am certain, remain some who are unconvinced by the above argument. Sure, sameness relations are required by the causal theory, but, no, they need not be cross-world relations or carry essentialist import. I do not think such a view can be defended; however, I have a separate argument for those who are unconvinced, one that is less controversial and has a weaker conclusion. Nonetheless, it quite compromises the causal theory of reference in the direction of empiricism. Actually, it is too simple to be called an argument—perhaps it should just be called a point. It is this: Even if the causal theory proper does not presuppose essentialism, it does presuppose essentialism if it is to be an account of reference to modally extended entities. This is trivial—we cannot refer to modally extended entities if there are none. But most of our terms *do* refer to modally extended entities. This is not trivial, but it seems just plain true.[33] It

---

[33]Two points for those to whom this seems a bold claim. First, we seem to be able to speak counterfactually about just about everything; indeed, we have to introduce a special 'world-slice' terminology in order to talk about things that could (do) not exist in other possible situations. Second, consider that bachelorhood is a modally extended entity. Analytic truths of the form '*F*'s are *G*' are about *F*'s, and, as these truths are necessary, *F*-hood must be modally extended. One may wonder whether we should be speaking of entities here rather than words—why not just say that most

will certainly be accepted by those who accept necessities *a posteriori*, which includes most causal theorists, and, at any rate, almost everyone agrees that there are true statements of the form 'Necessarily *P*'[34] that are not just truths of logic. Thus, if the causal theory is to be an account of the majority of our terms, it must be an account of reference to modally extended entities and, as such, requires essentialism for its truth.

The causal theory presupposes essentialism. But we have seen that the only acceptable form of essentialism is nominal essentialism, since real essentialism requires real necessity. And since nominal essences are, by definition, determined by our conventions, and the claim that we have these conventions is the heart of empiricist semantics, we see that the causal theory of reference cannot be true if empiricist semantics is not. Beyond the fact that empiricist semantics is true, we have this additional, more structural reason to think that the causal theory of reference must be compatible with empiricism. Again, this highlights the self-defeating nature of emphasizing the radical departure of causal theories from their predecessors; any causal theorist who wants to reasonably defend his theory must be willing to drop that historical claim.

This establishes my major contentions of this chapter: first, that the basic empiricist semantic claim is correct, and, second, that not only would the truth of the causal theory fail to overturn the empiricist view, but the causal theorist needs to be able to accommodate this view if his theory is to even possibly be true. But there is another interesting consequence of our most recent inquiry. When we see the need of the causal theory to be able to accommodate basic empiricist

---

terms are such that they may be the subject terms of necessary truths? I doubt that there is a real issue here; however, I discuss the contrast between the semantic and metaphysical understandings below.

[34]'Necessarily' is used here 'in its widest sense'.

semantics, we ought to take quite seriously the possibility that causal theories *can* be so accommodating, that the positive account of reference offerred by causal theorists does not require that they take a 'these are our opponents' attitude towards empiricist semantics, and that, in brief, our discovery of the need for the causal theory to accommodate empiricism does not show that the causal theory is false. At least on the face of it, any reasonable causal theorist faced with the fact that his theory is either compatible with empiricism or that it is false will try to explain how the former can be the case. Unless one's theory is of no intrinsic interest, one generally opts for truth over historical place. What I should like to do now, then, is to explain how it is that we might understand the causal theory so that it is compatible with empiricist semantics and, finally, to give a rough sketch of what such a theory might look like.

Two Versions of the Causal Theory

We know that causal theorists sometimes claim that if their theory is true, then empiricist semantic theories are false. This is no doubt true if we think of empiricist theories that essentially require that most of our terms have analytic definitions that constitute their intensions and determine their reference, or extensions. But we have put such theories to one side and are thinking of empiricism as fundamentally the position that we have conventional, individuating features in language that play a central role in the determination of reference. Now, even if it is so understood, there are certain to be some causal theorists who still believe their theory is incompatible with empiricism. Is there anything in their positive account to bear this out?

This will depend on how we understand what the causal theory claims, and there are, for our purposes, two possibilities here. The first we might call 'the extreme causal theory'. This is the view, which might also be called the 'full-blooded' view, according to which causal relations (of the right sort) between words and things are *all there is* to reference (or at least, to 'first' reference—reference by others requires (causal) acquisition from others with the ability to refer; ultimately, however, this will still boil down to causal relations between speakers and objects). This view *is* incompatible with even basic empiricism, for it entails that there is *no* important conventional element in the determination of reference—there are only causal relations. The second view, which we might call 'the modest causal theory', makes a less sweeping claim. Just as the basic empiricist position claims only that individuating conventions must be part of the story, so the modest causal theory claims only that causal relations between utterances of words and things in the world must also be part of the story. Since there is no obvious reason why causal relations and individuating conventions cannot be fit into a single picture, there is no obvious reason to think that the modest causal theory is incompatible with the basic empiricist view. On first consideration, one may think that there is no reason to want to so accommodate empiricism; one might think this if (1) one failed to see the causal theory's commitment to essentialism, (2) one failed to see the implausibility of real essentialism, and thus the need of essentialists to believe that we have individuating conventions, or (3) one misunderstood what is basic to empiricism. But whether or not one sees the need here, unless one finds strong reason to prefer the extreme to the modest causal theory, a causal theorist need not find his view wholly incompatible with empiricism. It is far from clear that the considerations that have led people to causal theories give them any more reason to believe the extreme rather than the modest theory. I enter here my speculation that the actual reasons are independent of considerations internal to the positive account and reside instead in negative beliefs fueled by (1) and (2) above; whether or not this is so, it remains that the belief that causal relations are important and that most terms do not have analytic definitions does not give one any reason to accept the extreme as opposed to the modest theory.

It is worth noting that we can now clear up a possible misconception of what is involved in the claim that the causal theory is either false or compatible with empiricist semantics. What is at stake is not whether some view—the causal theory—stands in a certain logical relation to another view, but rather how we are to interpret the title 'The Causal Theory'. There are two candidates, one of which is compatible with empiricism (the modest view) and the other of which is not (the extreme view). Our interest, then, is not in discerning a logical fact so that we can determine whether the causal theory might be true—we know all the facts about compatibility that are relevant here—but in pointing out the differing implications of two ways in which the causal theory might be understood, and, of course, the fact that causal theorists cannot have everything they want on *any* understanding.

A Modest Outline

Given that, so long as one is not an extreme causal theorist, one may accept both a causal theory and basic empiricism, we might now ask what such a semantic theory looks like, that is, a theory that emphasizes both causal relations between speakers and extralinguistic items, and conventional principles of individuation. Since we have said nothing against causal theories *per se*, except by way of extricating their tacit assumption, we might try to see how far we can go in saying just what causal theorists want to say, bringing general principles of individuation into play only where they are required to make that tacit assumption (essentialism) true.[35] This is not the only way the views can be reconciled,

[35]It is crucial to bear in mind that the assumption of essentialism we have

but I think that any 'hybrid' theory must look roughly like this. On such an approach, I think we can tell a fully coherent and plausible story. This story will be at least as plausible as causal theories so far presented have been, for it is the same story, different only in its addition of a conventional element that we now know to be both (1) required by any true semantic theory and (2) required for the truth of an assumption internal to the causal theory in particular. Further, insofar as the causal theory and the empiricist view are the two most discussed and (apparently) most plausible accounts of reference, this hybrid view, aside from modeling a reconciliation between the views, has a good claim to being (despite its roughness) the most plausible view, inasmuch as it accommodates everything causal theorists want to say (except for their denial of the empiricist claim), as well as accommodating the basic insight that underlies empiricism, without a commitment to analytic definitions for all terms, the commitment to which has been the focal point of anti-empiricist criticism. Again, however, my basic purpose is not primarily to present a worked-out theory of reference for which there are compelling arguments, but to show how causal theorists can accommodate basic empiricism, as well as to show (roughly) how general principles of individuation can figure in an account of reference (since we know they do, if there are not more particular analytic definitions). If, though, there must be conventional principles of individuation, and if the arguments given on behalf of causal theories have some force, then there is good reason to think that the truth about reference must look something like this.

---

discovered is not (need not be) an assumption of *real* essentialism. Thus, the expression 'makes essentialism come out true' is not so odd as it looks—for nominal essentialism just *is* the view that there are essences (and thus that essentialism is true) because of the conventional decisions of sentient beings. Again, insofar as causal theorists require real essentialism (as they will if they deny any important role to conventions), they cannot hope to have a true theory.

As causal theorists do (though not in this way), we may divide the theory of reference into two parts, a theory of reference in acquisition (origination), which explains how a word first gains reference, and a theory of reference in transfer, which explains how other tokens of a word-type have the reference they do.[36] Nothing said so far cuts in any way against the theory of reference in transfer advocated by causal theorists. Once there is a referential connection between a word and (typically) an extralinguistic object, other people can use tokens of the word with the same reference if their use of the word is 'grounded' in other people's referring uses. Thus, a Hungarian with no knowledge of American history at all can ask, after overhearing a conversation between two Americans, 'Who was Abraham Lincoln?' and be asking about our sixteenth president. His question is about Lincoln because he got the expression 'Abraham Lincoln' from people who were using it to talk about Lincoln. To use the jargon, he has 'borrowed' the ability to refer to Lincoln with this name from the people he overheard.

Doubtless, more needs to be said about the conditions under which such borrowing has successfully occurred. The basic idea is clear, however, and it is important. For if such borrowing occurs, as it undoubtedly does, then it is not the case, as claimed by Locke and others, that each speaker must determine for himself the meaning (and thus the reference) of (each of) his words. Not only need one not determine for himself such meanings, but one need not even try to figure out what meaning others have associated with the term. One need only get it and use it. Thus, there really is 'reference in transfer' and not merely 'reference in acquisition'; we can make use of other people's ability to refer, and need not figure out their meaning and associate it with our use of a term in order to use that term and have it have the same reference as it did for them. Whatever else is involved in such

[36]Apologies to Robert Nozick.

borrowing, the fact that someone has causally acquired the term from another speaker undoubtedly plays a central role in determining the reference of the term for that (the acquiring) speaker.[37]

Now, as I say, nothing in our discussion cuts against this part of causal theories, and we have excellent reason to accept (at least in part) a causal analysis of reference in transfer. It must be noted, however, that nothing in empiricist semantics requires empiricists to be at all troubled by this. While many empiricists have treated reference in transfer as but a special case of reference in acquisition (insofar as they treat of the former at all), their views about reference in acquisition certainly do not require this. One may take a hard empiricist line, thinking that nearly all terms gain their reference through analytically associated intensions, and still think that speakers may borrow reference from one another as causal theorists propose. Nothing in the basic theory of reference, explaining how terms first acquire their referents, precludes this. Thus, while we ought, I think, to accept this feature of the causal theory, it is erroneous to think, as has often been suggested, that the considerations supporting this—for instance, the fact that most speakers cannot produce uniquely identifying descriptions underlying their uses of names—cut at all against anything fundamental[38] in empiricist semantics.[39]

This brings us to what is more fundamental, the theory of reference in acquisition. While we have not had to modify or add to anything causal theorists say about reference in trans-

---

[37]See Kripke, *Naming and Necessity*, Lecture Two, and Devitt, *Designation* (New York: Columbia University Press, 1981).

[38]And by 'fundamental' here, I mean something more robust than what I have called 'the basic empiricist semantic claim'—as can be seen through the above remarks about 'hard empiricism'.

[39]One finds this suggestion, for instance, in Kripke, *Naming and Necessity*, Lecture One, Putnam, "The Meaning of 'Meaning'," pp. 218–38, and Devitt, *Designation*.

fer, we cannot similarly let everything here pass by without comment. As we have described it so far, the causal theory claims that reference is a causal relation between words and items in the world. While it is not at all essential to the causal theory, it is useful to view 'baptism' as a model of the establishing of a referential connection. Some feature of the world is focused upon, with or without the help of an identifying description, and some word is introduced to name that feature. In Putnam's example, someone holds up a glass of water, points to it, and says 'We will call this 'water'' ('Whatever is relevantly like this is water'). As causal theorists like to describe it, this ceremony establishes a referential tie between the word 'water' and a certain natural kind, in this case, the chemical kind H_2O. There is no analytically specified set of necessary and sufficient conditions that constitutes the definition of 'water'. Even if some description were used to pick out the object, say, 'the liquid in this glass', it would still not be true that 'The liquid in this glass is water' was analytic, since, for one thing, it is only contingently true. The glass in question could have contained grape juice, vodka, or Mongolian fire oil. And it has been argued, with some success among members of the philosophic community, that reflection upon our counterfactual intuitions supports the claim that the link between our words, like 'water', and features of the world, like H_2O, is direct: the word refers to the kind, whether or not the kind satisfies descriptions that anyone associates with the term.

Now, this is fine as far as it goes. However, if the major contentions of this book are correct, then this story, as presented, skates over certain vital aspects of the situation. As causal theorists like to talk, it is as if, quite independently of any cognitive choice, there are neatly individuated features of the world out there waiting to receive names. We need only attach the labels. If this were true, there would certainly be no need to have any sorts of analytic connections between expressions in order to refer to the features of the world that we do; whether we have such conventions or not would simply be an empirical issue, and this, the impression is given, is the issue over which empiricists and causal theorists are in disagreement.

However, as I have argued, analytic connections do not appear in empiricist semantics as so much extra baggage. If empiricist metaphysics is correct regarding necessity and individuation, as I have argued it is, then the semantic view that we have conventional principles of individuation is not a bit of social speculation. There must be some such principles if we are to have the referential connections that both empiricists and causal theorists agree that we do have. There are not independently individuated kinds and things out there waiting to be labeled. We need first to divide the world up. We thus need conventional principles of individuation, and this is what gets passed over in typical expositions of causal theories of reference.

As we have seen, this presents no critical problem for causal theorists. There is no principled reason why they cannot accept such conventional principles. They need not talk as if real essentialism were true, as if conventional decisions play no role. It is likely that the reason they do talk this way is that they do not see any problem here; however, the fact that there *is* a problem, that real essentialism is untenable, does not show that there is a problem for them. The only real problem is that since they do not typically see the problem, and talk like real essentialists, they leave the individuating conventions out of their account and thus create the false impression (which they might believe, making them extreme causal theorists) that there is no need for them.

With this much clear, we now want to see how conventional principles of individuation may enter most innocuously into the sort of account of reference in acquisition that causal theorists want to give. The causal theorist wants to say that we can point to a glass of liquid and say, 'Whatever is the same stuff as this is water'. Our metaphysical reflections have shown that, independently of our conventions, no definite sense can be given to the notion of 'the same stuff as this'.[40] We need, then, to have our reference-fixing (whether through baptism or a more gradual, everyday introduction of a term) either *include* or be *annexed to* some generally specified principle of individuation to determine the relevant respects of sameness for the type of entity to which we want to refer.

A reference-fixing would *include* a principle of individuation if it were somehow conceived to be a part of the process that the respects of sameness were actually specified, as might be modeled on Putnam's ostender saying 'Whatever is like this in chemical microstructure' or 'Whatever has the same underlying causally important features as this'. A reference-fixing would be *annexed to* a general principle if we thought of ourselves as having antecedently determined to have a class of words referring to bits of the world according to, say, their chemical or otherwise deepest explanatory features, and then introduced 'water' more explicitly like the ostender—'Whatever is of the same kind (natural kind, chemical kind) as this is water'. Insofar as we believe that wherever there is a term for an entity or kind whose essence is 'discovered', there are other terms and entities of the same sort,[41] then there does not seem to be much to choose in theory between 'including' or 'annexing' views of the relation between reference-fixings and principles of individuation. In either case, it is conventionally determined, again only indirectly (generally), what the respect of sameness is for things of this sort (this is what makes the theory empiricist), but it is, finally, empirically determined just what in particular the sameness-making features are (for example, H_2O). We have,

---

[40]Or, again, no *determinate* sense, if one thinks the problem is rather that there are *too many* things and kinds. Remarks of this sort are to be found repeatedly in Wittgenstein's later writings. What follows can be read so as to accommodate either of these ways of understanding the problem.

[41]This is the speculation I have earlier remarked upon in proposing that there are *general* principles of individuation.

as outlined in Chapter Two, necessary truths that are *a posteriori*, but the modal aspects of these are grounded in our conventions.

It must be emphasized that what is conventional is not just which class of individuating principles a term comes to be 'annexed to' or has its reference-fixing associated with, but what the general principles of individuation are. Many causal theorists recognize that they cannot just ostend, but need to say 'natural kind' or 'liquid', to determine (in one respect) the relevant respect of the thing they are using as an exemplar. This, they may agree, is conventional, but it involves them in no *interesting* conventional elements. However, in the account I have offered—and, again, in any account that can be true—the principles of individuation are themselves conventional. It is not just that 'cat', say, gets (conventionally) annexed to the natural-kind principle, but the principle itself conventionally determines boundaries, here according to important underlying features. Thus, it is quite amenable to me if causal theorists think that the account here outlined is just like their account. For with these general principles of individuation, there can be no doubt that this theory is in the empiricist tradition, encompassing the basic empiricist semantic view, and only moving definitions to a more abstract level. If it is also acceptable to causal theorists—and it seems that the only reason it might not be is if those theorists are wedded to the extreme view, which we know by now to be self-defeating (or at least false)—then we have successfully seen how a causal theory can accommodate the basic empiricist semantic view, and that the commitment to essentialism is not a problem for causal theorists.

Conclusion

As in the metaphysical case, the empiricist can applaud and acknowledge the insights of recent philosophers of language.

He need not, however, accept the claim that these insights force us to a radical and fundamental revision of more traditional theories. Empiricist theories can accommodate—indeed, if my arguments have been correct, accommodate best—these recent findings. We ought not to think that we have been thrust into a new philosophical age, nor ought we to think that empiricist metaphysics and semantics can be maintained only at the cost of ignorance or hard-headedness. On the contrary, empiricism can be abandoned only at such cost: for such a move requires either overestimating the consequences of admittedly interesting insights or underestimating the resources and fundamental bases of empiricism. New insights are the stuff of philosophical progress. But progress does not always require revolution.

This leads me to a final remark. If the insights that have helped make plausible both the necessary *a posteriori* and the causal theory of reference are reasonably called 'realist', and if, as I have argued, they are best understood as consonant with—indeed, as incorporated into—empiricist accounts, then perhaps realism and empiricism are not the opposed frameworks they are sometimes supposed to be. While there are, without doubt, localized disputes, when we look at the big picture, empiricists and realists may see things quite the same.

Bibliography

Adams, R. 1971. "Has It Been Proved That All Existence Is Contingent?" *American Philosophical Quarterly* 8:284–91.
———. 1979. "Primitive Thisness and Primitive Identity." *Journal of Philosophy* 76:5–26.
———. 1983. "Divine Necessity." *Journal of Philosophy* 80:741–51.
Aristotle. *Categories*. Revised Oxford Translation. In J. Barnes, ed., *Complete Works of Aristotle*. Princeton: Princeton University Press (1984).
———. *Metaphysics*. Revised Oxford Translation. In ibid.
Ayers, M. 1981. "Locke versus Aristotle on Natural Kinds." *Journal of Philosophy* 78:247–72.
Bonjour, L. 1976. "The Coherence Theory of Empirical Knowledge." *Philosophical Studies* 30:281–312.
———. 1985. *The Structure of Empirical Knowledge*. Cambridge: Harvard University Press.
Boyd, R. 1980. "Scientific Realism and Naturalistic Epistemology." *Philosophy of Science Association* 2:613–62.
———. 1983. "Natural Kinds, Homeostasis and the Limits of Essentialism." Unpublished.
Brink, D. 1984. "Moral Realism and the Sceptical Arguments from Disagreement and Queerness." *Australasian Journal of Philosophy* 62:111–25.
———. 1989. *Moral Realism and the Foundations of Ethics*. Cambridge: Cambridge University Press.
Brody, B. 1980. *Identity and Essence*. Princeton: Princeton University Press.
Butchvarov, P. 1977. "Identity." In P. French, T. Uehling, and H.

Wettstein, eds., *Contemporary Perspectives in the Philosophy of Language*. Minneapolis: University of Minnesota Press, 1979a.

——. 1979. *Being qua Being*. Bloomington: Indiana University Press.

Carnap, R. 1947. *Meaning and Necessity*. Chicago: University of Chicago Press.

Cartwright, R. 1968. "Some Remarks on Essentialism." *Journal of Philosophy* 65:615–26.

Cassim, Q. 1986. "Science and Essence." *Philosophy* 61:95–107.

Coppock, P. 1984. Review of *Reference and Essence*, by N. Salmon. *Journal of Philosophy* 81:261–70.

Davidson, D., and G. Harman, eds. 1972. *Semantics of Natural Language*. Dordrecht: D. Reidel.

Devitt, M. 1981. *Designation*. New York: Columbia University Press.

——. 1983. "Dummett's Anti-Realism." *Journal of Philosophy* 80:73–99.

Donnellan, K. 1966. "Reference and Definite Descriptions." *Philosophical Review* 75:281–304. Reprinted in J. Rosenberg and C. Travis, eds., *Readings in the Philosophy of Language* (Englewood Cliffs, N.J.: Prentice-Hall, 1971) and in S. Schwartz, ed., *Naming, Necessity and Natural Kinds* (Ithaca: Cornell University Press, 1977).

——. 1968. "Putting Humpty Dumpty Together Again." *Philosophical Review* 77:203–15.

——. 1972. "Proper Names and Identifying Descriptions." In D. Davidson and G. Harman, eds., *Semantics of Natural Language* (Dordrecht: D. Reidel, 1972).

——. 1974a. "Speaking of Nothing." *Philosophical Review* 83:3–31. Reprinted in S. Schwartz, ed., *Naming, Necessity and Natural Kinds* (Ithaca: Cornell University Press, 1977).

——. 1974b. "Rigid Designators, Natural Kinds and Individuals." Unpublished.

——. 1977. "The Contingent *A Priori* and Rigid Designators." In P. French, T. Uehling, and H. Wettstein, eds., *Contemporary Perspectives in the Philosophy of Language*. Minneapolis: University of Minnesota Press, 1979a.

——. 1978. "Speaker Reference, Descriptions and Anaphora." In French, Uehling, and Wettstein 1979a.

——. 1983. "Kripke and Putnam on Natural Kind Terms." In C. Ginet and S. Shoemaker, eds., *Knowledge and Mind*. New York: Oxford University Press.

Dummett, M. 1975. "What Is a Theory of Meaning?" In S. Guttenplan, ed., *Mind and Language*. Oxford: Clarendon Press.

——. 1976. "What is a Theory of Meaning (II)?" In G. Evans and J.

McDowell, eds., *Truth and Meaning*. Oxford: Oxford University Press.

———. 1980. *Truth and Other Enigmas*. Cambridge: Harvard University Press.

Farrell, R. 1981. "Metaphysical Necessity Is Not Logical Necessity." *Philosophical Studies* 37:141–53.

Field, H. 1972. "Tarski's Theory of Truth." *Journal of Philosophy* 69:247–72.

———. 1973. "Theory Change and the Indeterminacy of Reference." *Journal of Philosophy* 70:462–81.

———. 1974. "Quine and the Correspondence Theory." *Philosophical Review* 83:200–228.

———. 1984. "Is Mathematical Knowledge Just Logical Knowledge?" *Philosophical Review* 93:509–54.

Fitch, G. 1976. "Are There Necessary *A Posteriori* Truths?" *Philosophical Studies* 30:243–47.

Foot, P. 1972. "Morality as a System of Hypothetical Imperatives." *Philosophical Review* 81:305–16.

Forbes, G. 1980. "Origin and Identity." *Philosophical Studies* 37:353–62.

———. 1981. "On the Philosophical Basis of Essentialist Theories." *Journal of Philosophical Logic* 10:73–99.

———. 1985. *The Metaphysics of Modality*. Oxford and New York: Clarendon Press.

Frege, G. 1892. "On Sense and Reference." *See* Frege 1980.

———. 1980. *Translations from the Philosophical Writings of Gottlob Frege*. Ed. P. T. Geach and M. Black. Totowa, N.J.: Rowman and Littlefield.

French, P., T. Uehling, and H. Wettstein, eds. 1979a. *Contemporary Perspectives in the Philosophy of Language*. Minneapolis: University of Minnesota Press.

———. 1979b. *Midwest Studies in Philosophy IV: Metaphysics*. Minneapolis: University of Minnesota Press.

———. 1986. *Midwest Studies in Philosophy XI: Studies in Essentialism*. Minneapolis: University of Minnesota Press.

Gibbard, A. 1975. "Contingent Identity." *Journal of Philosophical Logic* 4:187–222.

Goodman, N. 1965. *Fact, Fiction and Forecast*. 2d ed. Indianapolis: Bobbs-Merrill.

Goosen, W. 1977. "Underlying Trait Terms." In S. Schwartz, ed., *Naming, Necessity and Natural Kinds*. Ithaca: Cornell University Press, 1977.

Grandy, R. 1975. "Stuff and Things." *Synthese* 31:479–85.
Grice, P. (with P. Strawson). 1956. "In Defense of a Dogma." *Philosophical Review* 65:141–58. Reprinted in J. Rosenberg and C. Travis, eds., *Readings in the Philosophy of Language* (Englewood Cliffs, N.J.: Prentice-Hall, 1971).
———. 1957. "Meaning." *Philosophical Review* 66:377–88. Reprinted in J. Rosenberg and C. Travis, eds., *Readings in the Philosophy of Language* (Englewood Cliffs, N.J.: Prentice-Hall, 1971).
Hanson, N. R. 1958. *Patterns of Discovery.* Cambridge: Cambridge University Press.
Harman, G. 1973. *Thought.* Princeton: Princeton University Press.
Hirsch, E. 1982. *The Concept of Identity.* Oxford: Oxford University Press.
Hume, D. 1739. *A Treatise on Human Nature.* Ed. L. A. Selby-Bigge. Oxford: Clarendon Press, 1978.
Kant, I. 1781. *Critique of Pure Reason.* Translated by Norman Kemp Smith. New York: St. Martin's Press, 1965.
Kaplan, D. 1967. "Trans-World Heir Lines." In M. Loux, ed., *The Possible and the Actual.* Ithaca: Cornell University Press, 1979.
———. 1970. "Dthat." In P. French, T. Uehling, and H. Wettstein, eds., *Contemporary Perspectives in the Philosophy of Language.* Minneapolis: University of Minnesota Press, 1979a.
———. 1973. "On the Logic of Demonstratives." In P. French, T. Uehling, and H. Wettstein, eds., *Contemporary Perspectives in the Philosophy of Language.* Minneapolis: University of Minnesota Press, 1979a.
Kim, J. 1977. "Perception and Reference without Causality." *Journal of Philosophy* 74:606–20.
Kitcher, P. S. 1978. "Theories, Theorists and Theoretical Change." *Philosophical Review* 87:519–47.
———. 1980. "*A Priori* Knowledge." *Philosophical Review* 89:3–23.
Kripke, S. 1971. "Identity and Necessity." In S. Schwartz, ed., *Naming, Necessity and Natural Kinds.* Ithaca: Cornell University Press, 1977.
———. 1972. "Naming and Necessity." In D. Davidson and G. Harman, eds., *Semantics of Natural Language.* Dordrecht: D. Reidel, 1972. Published as a book, Cambridge: Harvard University Press, 1980. All references are to the book page numbers.
———. 1979. "Speaker's Reference and Semantic Reference." In P. French, T. Uehling, and H. Wettstein, eds., *Contemporary Perspectives in the Philosophy of Language.* Minneapolis: University of Minnesota Press, 1979a.

———. 1982. *Wittgenstein on Rules and Private Language*. Cambridge: Harvard University Press.

Kuhn, T. S. 1962. *The Structure of Scientific Revolutions*. Chicago: University of Chicago Press.

Laycock, H. 1972. "Some Questions of Ontology." *Philosophical Review* 81:3–42.

Lewis, C. I. 1944. "The Modes of Meaning." In L. Linsky, ed., *Semantics and the Philosophy of Language*. Urbana: University of Illinois Press, 1952.

Lewis, D. 1969. *Convention*. Cambridge: Harvard University Press.

———. 1983. *Philosophical Papers Vol. 1*. Oxford: Oxford University Press.

———. 1984. "Putnam's Paradox." *Australasian Journal of Philosophy* 62:221–36.

———. 1986. *On the Plurality of Worlds*. Oxford and New York: Basil Blackwell.

Lewy, C. 1976. *Meaning and Modality*. Cambridge: Cambridge University Press.

Linsky, L., ed. 1952. *Semantics and the Philosophy of Language*. Urbana: University of Illinois Press.

Locke, J. 1689. *Essay Concerning Human Understanding*. Ed. P. H. Nidditch. Oxford: Clarendon Press, 1975.

Loux, M., ed. 1979. *The Possible and the Actual*. Ithaca: Cornell University Press.

Mackie, J. 1974a. "Locke's Anticipation of Kripke." *Analysis* 34:177–80.

———. 1974b. "*De* What *Re* Is *De Re* Modality?" *Journal of Philosophy* 71:551–61.

———. 1977. *Ethics: Inventing Right and Wrong*. New York: Penguin Books.

Marcus, R. B. 1947. "The Identity of Individuals in a Strict Functional Calculus of Second Order." *Journal of Symbolic Logic* 12:12–25.

———. 1967. "Essentialism in Modal Logic." *Nous* 1:91–96.

Mates, B. 1951. "Analytic Sentences." *Philosophical Review* 60:525–34.

McBride, R. R. 1983. "Striped Leopards and Spotted Tigers: A New Realist Look at Biological Taxonomy." *Journal of Large Animals* 11:104–31.

McGinn, C. 1976. "On the Necessity of Origin." *Journal of Philosophy* 73:127–35.

———. 1981. "The Mechanism of Reference." *Synthese* 49:157–86.

Pap, A. 1958. *Semantics and Necessary Truth*. New Haven: Yale University Press.

Parfit, D. 1971. "Personal Identity." *Philosophical Review* 80:3–27.
——. 1984. *Reasons and Persons*. Oxford: Oxford University Press.
Parsons, T. 1969. "Essentialism and Quantified Modal Logic." *Philosophical Review* 78:35–52.
Plantinga, A. 1970. "World and Essence." *Philosophical Review* 79:461–92.
——. 1974. *The Nature of Necessity*. Oxford: Clarendon Press.
Price, M. S. 1982. "On the Non-Necessity of Origin." *Canadian Journal of Philosophy* 12:33–45.
Putnam, H. 1962. "It Ain't Necessarily So." *See* Putnam 1975b.
——. 1966. "The Analytic and the Synthetic." *See* Putnam 1975c.
——. 1970. "Is Semantics Possible?" *See* Putnam 1975c. Also in S. Schwartz, ed., *Naming, Necessity and Natural Kinds*. Ithaca: Cornell University Press, 1977.
——. 1975a. "The Meaning of 'Meaning'." *See* Putnam 1975c.
——. 1975b. *Philosophical Papers I: Mathematics, Matter and Method*. Cambridge: Cambridge University Press.
——. 1975c. *Philosophical Papers II: Mind, Language and Reality*. Cambridge: Cambridge University Press.
——. 1976. "'Two Dogmas' Revisited." *See* Putnam 1983.
——. 1978. *Meaning and the Moral Sciences*. Boston: Routledge and Kegan Paul.
——. 1981. *Reason, Truth and History*. New York: Cambridge University Press.
——. 1983. *Philosophical Papers III: Realism and Reason*. Cambridge: Cambridge University Press.
Quine, W. V. O. 1936. "Truth by Convention." *See* Quine 1966.
——. 1951. "Two Dogmas of Empiricism." *See* Quine 1953. Also in J. Rosenberg and C. Travis, eds., *Readings in the Philosophy of Language*. Englewood Cliffs, N.J.: Prentice-Hall, 1971.
——. 1953. *From a Logical Point of View*. Cambridge: Harvard University Press.
——. 1960. *Word and Object*. Cambridge: MIT Press.
——. 1966. *The Ways of Paradox*. Cambridge: Harvard University Press.
——. 1969. *Ontological Relativity*. New York: Columbia University Press.
Rawls, J. 1971. *A Theory of Justice*. Cambridge: Harvard University Press.
Rosenberg, J. and Travis, C., eds. 1971. *Readings in the Philosophy of Language*. Englewood Cliffs, N.J.: Prentice-Hall.
Russell, B. 1905. "On Denoting." *Mind* 14:479–93. *See also* Russell 1956.

———. 1911. "Knowledge by Acquaintance and Knowledge by Description." In Russell, *Mysticism and Logic*. London: Longmans, Green.

———. 1918. "The Philosophy of Logical Atomism." *See* Russell 1956.

———. 1956. *Logic and Knowledge*. Ed. R. C. Marsh. London: George Allen and Unwin.

Salmon, N. 1979. "How *Not* to Derive Essentialism from the Theory of Reference." *Journal of Philosophy* 76:703–25.

———. 1981. *Reference and Essence*. Princeton: Princeton University Press.

Schiffer, S. 1973. *Meaning*. Oxford: Oxford University Press.

Schwartz, S., ed. 1977. *Naming, Necessity and Natural Kinds*. Ithaca: Cornell University Press.

Sellars, W. 1956. "Empiricism and the Philosophy of Mind." In H. Feigl and M. Scriven, eds., *Minnesota Studies in the Philosophy of Science*. Vol. 1. Minneapolis: University of Minnesota Press.

Shoemaker, S. 1979. "Identity, Properties and Causality." In P. French, T. Uehling, and H. Wettstein, eds., *Midwest Studies in Philosophy IV: Metaphysics*. Minneapolis: University of Minnesota Press, 1979b.

Smith, A.D. 1984. "Rigidity and Scope." *Mind* 93:177–93.

Stalnaker, R. (with R. Thomason). 1968. "Modality and Reference." *Nous* 2:359–72.

———. 1976. "Propositions." In A. MacKay and D. Merrill, eds., *Issues in the Philosophy of Language*. New Haven: Yale University Press.

———. 1977. "Complex Predicates." *Monist* 60:327–39.

———. 1979. "Anti-Essentialism." In P. French, T. Uehling, and H. Wettstein, eds., *Midwest Studies in Philosophy IV: Metaphysics*. Minneapolis: University of Minnesota Press, 1979b.

———. 1987. *Inquiry*. Cambridge: MIT Press.

Strawson, P. F. 1959. *Individuals*. London: Methuen.

Stroud, B. 1965. "Wittgenstein and Logical Necessity." *Philosophical Review* 74:504–18.

Teller, P. 1975. "Essential Properties: Some Problems and Conjectures." *Journal of Philosophy* 72:233–48.

Van Fraassen, B. 1977. "The Only Necessity Is Verbal Necessity." *Journal of Philosophy* 74:71–85.

———. 1980. *The Scientific Image*. Oxford: Clarendon Press.

White, M. 1949. "The Analytic and the Synthetic: An Untenable Dualism." In L. Linsky, ed., *Semantics and the Philosophy of Language*. Urbana: University of Illinois Press, 1952.

Wiggins, D. 1979. "Ayer on Monism, Pluralism and Essence." In G. MacDonald, ed., *Perception and Identity*. Ithaca: Cornell University Press.

———. 1980. *Sameness and Substance*. Cambridge: Harvard University Press.

Wittgenstein, L. 1921. *Tractatus Logico-Philosophicus*. London: Routledge & Kegan Paul, 1961.

———. 1929. "Some Remarks on Logical Form." *Proceedings of the Aristotelian Society*, Supp. vol. 9:162–71.

———. 1933. *Philosophical Grammar*. Berkeley: University of California Press, 1978.

———. 1935. *The Blue and Brown Books*. New York: Basil Blackwell, 1958.

———. 1948. *Zettel*. Berkeley: University of California Press, 1970.

———. 1949. *Philosophical Investigations*. New York: MacMillan, 1953.

Zemach, E. 1976. "Putnam's Theory on the Reference of Substance Terms." *Journal of Philosophy* 73:116–27.

Index

Library of Congress Cataloging-in-Publication Data

Sidelle, Alan, 1960–
  Necessity, essence, and individuation : a defense of conventionalism /
Alan Sidelle.
    p.   cm.
  Bibliography: p.
  Includes index.
  ISBN 0-8014-2166-7 (alk. paper)
  1. Convention (Philosophy) 2. Necessity (Philosophy) 3. Realism. 4.
Essence (Philosophy) 5. Individuation. 6. Empiricism. I. Title
B809.15.S56   1989   146'.44—dc20   89-7122